P9-DNA-985

INDUSTRIALISM AND THE POPES

Industrialism and The Popes

A STUDY MADE UNDER THE AUSPICES OF
THE DEPARTMENT OF SOCIOLOGY
SAINT LOUIS UNIVERSITY
WITH SPECIAL EMPHASIS ON THE
INDUSTRY COUNCIL PLAN

Mary Lois Eberdt, C.H.M., Ph.D.

Chairman, Division of Social Sciences
Marycrest College

AND

Gerald J. Schnepp, S.M., Ph.D.

Associate Professor of Sociology
Saint Louis University

Foreword by Most Reverend ROBERT E. LUCEY, S.T.D.

Archbishop of San Antonio

P. J. KENEDY & SONS · NEW YORK

CUM PERMISSU SUPERIORUM

NIHIL OBSTAT: William T. O'Connor
Censor Deputatus

IMPRIMATUR: ✠ Ralph L. Hayes
Bishop of Davenport

Davenport
October 30, 1952

PEACE IS THE WORK
OF JUSTICE.

✠

Motto of Pope Pius XII

Contents

PART ONE

THE INDUSTRY COUNCIL PLAN

Its Necessity: Abuses in Present Economic System. Necessity for Reorganization.

Papal Insistence on Reform: Papal Appeal to Clergy. Papal Appeal to Groups. Papal Appeal to All. Those Who Ignore Papal Appeal.

PART TWO

SPECIFIC PRINCIPLES INVOLVED IN THE INDUSTRY COUNCIL PLAN

Present Society. True Nature of Organic Structure: *Unity; Function.* Responsibility of All for Co-operation.

Meaning and Function. Position of the State.

Stewardship of Wealth. Violation of Duties of
Stewardship.
Private Property: A Natural Right. Protection.
Right of All. Errors and Abuses. Duties of the
State.

Dignity of Labor: Value of Labor. Labor's
Function in the Divine Plan.
The Family: Position of the Family. Family
Living Wage. A Grave Responsibility. Reason
for Living Wage.
International Order: World Community.
Brotherhood in Fatherhood of God. Socio-
Economic Implications.

Foreword

In an extraordinary editorial[1] in that extraordinary journal—the German Catholic review *Wort und Wahrheit*, the writer observes,

> Catholics have a most disastrous tendency to cleave to the abstract and the generalized and to fight shy of the concrete and particular. We are everlastingly developing and repeating "principles" but can never make up our minds to apply them to reality—we do not even try to find such applications in our minds. Indeed, because we misunderstand them, they tend to bar our very entry to reality, for we merely see their *normative* and not their *creative* quality; we forget that these "principles" are literally "beginnings" and that they should not only guide our conduct but are *powers of truth which issue a perpetual challenge.* (*Italics ours.*)

This habit of principle-mongering is no monopoly of Germans. We of the United States must plead guilty to the same almost superstitious faith in the "power of ideas" or promulgation of principles, to the neglect of taking action on them, applying them to the social reality all about us. But there is one bright new exception to this prevailing impasse: the Industry Council Plan, which, though still in the theoretical or "paper" stage itself, yet represents a really tangible, practical, constructive, and reasonable

[1] "The Sleep of the Disciples," as translated in the *Dublin Review*, Third Quarter, 1952.

method of taking Christian social principles out of the realm of dry formalism and into the arena of working democracy, out of the "normative" into the "creative," out of thought into technique.

Yet the technique needs the thought, the practice needs the principle. The "challenge" needs the "powers of truth" behind it. Principles—or beginnings—do indeed come first; then comes the technical application (in this case the Industry Council Plan). But then the principles must again be stated—this time as documentation, corroboration, authority, justification for the technique so set up. That is the function of this book: to synthesize and organize all papal pronouncements that bear on the economic order of our day; to supply the "powers of truth" for the challenge accepted by those who have designed the Industry Council Plan.

This book will answer, as can no other existing work, the questions that will inevitably be fired at proponents of the Industry Council Plan when once it makes its way into the councils of labor and capital:—What is the authority for such-and-such premise or statement?—Where can we look for absolutes, certitudes, solid bases for our thinking?—Where, in short, lies truth? This book says, in effect: Go to the Popes. And it should be strongly emphasized that a statement is not true just because a Pope has said it, but rather a Pope has made the statement because it is true, it is *truth*—grounded in Divine, natural, and positive law.

Our authors, Sister Mary Lois Eherdt, C.H.M., and Gerald Schnepp, S.M. (himself one of the architects of the Industry Council Plan), have described and charted the features of the Plan in Chapter I of this book. It shall be my task simply to sketch in the background of social and economic disorder which inspired the papal texts under re-examination in the following pages.

These papal encyclicals and allocutions point out many defects in our economic order, but two are central: one a structural defect, the other functional. In the very structure, or machinery, of industrial life there is conflict. The bitter resentments, hostilities, and injustices frequently found in the relations of employers and employed are known to all. But, besides this feuding, many of the owning, managing class wage wars of extermination against their fellow capitalists, and the house of labor is divided, disorganized, and at times lacking in charity.

Before the right to collective bargaining was recognized by civil law the labor market was a battleground. It still is, to an alarming extent. Here the quarrel is about wages, hours of labor, and conditions of work. At first glance one might think that the interests of employer and employee are, and always will be, essentially at variance, since low wages and long hours mean more money for the owner, while the worker will always demand a larger share of the profits. But intelligent businessmen are now aware that generally low wages, dissatisfied workers, and unfavorable conditions of labor are bad for business in every segment of our economy. Conflict still remains, however, because collective bargaining is not synonymous with security and organized co-operation. The lack of organic unity is still apparent in strikes and in the use of economic power as a club to win a battle between opposing forces.

Owners of productive facilities not only quarrel with

their workers; but they sometimes carry on a quiet, devastating war, beyond the preserves of fair competition, among themselves. In some instances it is a question of the survival of the fittest—which means those who have the greatest power and the least conscience. Small businessmen often find the going pretty tough. They may be absorbed by a larger firm or just driven into bankruptcy.

A third area of conflict is the field of labor. At the moment there are more than sixty million employed persons in our country and only about one fourth of them are members of adequate labor unions. Unorganized workers often share in wage rates established by unions, but the great mass of wage earners who have so little bargaining power are a constant threat to the stability and progress of organized labor. Those who stand defenceless and alone in the labor market will usually work longer hours for less pay under worse conditions than will be accepted by members of a bona fide union. (And within legitimate unions themselves, there are all too many instances of power-politics, racketeering, and cold-blooded materialism—though this may be considered a moral problem rather than a structural defect.)

Here then is a major structural defect in the economic order: an almost complete lack of organic unity in the machinery of industrial and agricultural life. In itself this is sufficient to give us a bad social order, but a functional defect must also be noted—economic immorality. However well men may build the structure of industrial relations, the machinery will not operate smoothly if it is lubricated with the sand of immorality rather than with the good oil of justice and charity. Therefore, there must be a reform of morals.

Our Supreme Pontiffs have noted the organic disunity of social life and its immoralities. They have pronounced certain principles of a social and Christian character to heal the abuses and wounds of society. The moral law and its implications are within the competence of the Vicars of Christ. There is an obvious relationship between environment and salvation. When living conditions are poor, souls are lost. The good life here makes easier the acquisition of eternal life hereafter. The Church is determined to protect souls from an inhuman existence on earth wherein only heroes can survive.

If the principles of the good life are subject to the authority of the teaching Church, the precise application of these principles must be left to experts in various parts of the world. The Popes have not attempted to draw up a blueprint of the socio-economic order—they leave that to Christian economists and sociologists like our present authors. Thus it has come about that leading Catholic scholars propose the Industry Council Plan as a form of organized economic life in harmony with the papal program of social reconstruction.

In *Quadragesimo Anno* Pope Pius XI calls for a reorganization of the social economy and a reform of morals. He advocates organized industries and professions—occupational groups—which will be self-governing. Neither the structural nor the moral reform will be accomplished in the near future. Too many people will be against it. Catholics generally will support the idea of economic morality as they understand it, but many of them will not be enthusiastic about self-governing occupational groups. Yet more than sixty years ago the great Pope Leo XIII declared that a solution of the social question must be quickly found.

He defended the right of labor to organize. More than twenty years ago Pope Pius XI praised the achievements of labor unions and added: "May they set before themselves the task of preparing the way for those larger and more important guilds, industries and professions, and make every effort to bring them to realization" (*Quadragesimo Anno*). According to this Pontiff all workers and all owners should be organized jointly. Unfortunately, some of our people have not yet caught up in their social thinking with Pope Leo XIII. Just when they will catch up with Pope Pius XI is a question.

An opposition far more intransigent than that of certain Catholic groups is offered by those who do not even accept the validity of Christian principles. Their argument goes something like this:

"Christian principles are sterile and impotent. We have had them for two thousand years and the world is growing steadily worse. Religion cannot create the good life on earth. You Christians have tried and you have failed. You are so enamoured of the other world that you neglect the things by which men live. Your Church has no influence on public institutions and very little influence on the private life of man. In the face of unspeakable human misery, racial injustice, and economic slavery you have preached patience to persecuted, exploited, and desperate men. Instead of lifting them up to the more abundant life here and now you have given them vague promises of rewards and punishments in a life to come. You have tolerated the intolerable. You have been afraid of your own convictions because social justice is an agitator and social charity is a revolution.

"In the field of industrial relations your gospel has been impotent. In fact our so-called economic order has become so savage that one of your Christian leaders, Pope Pius XI, was constrained to cry out against it, saying: 'All economic life has become tragically hard, inexorable and cruel.' Where your gospel has been preached for centuries, the people have borne a yoke little better than slavery itself. And so in the fields of industry and agriculture your Church is outmoded and decrepit. Christian principles are sterile and impotent."

What answer do Catholics give to this indictment? The answer is slightly shopworn, but here it is: "Christian principles have not failed, but Christians have failed to make them work." It certainly is satisfying and consoling to know that we have the true principles of the good life received from an infallible teacher, but our record in making them effective is not too good. There are just too many Christians who have ignored, or never knew, the social teaching of their own religion. They are hardly worthy of the glorious name of Christian.

The life of man on earth is a warfare; too many of us have been poor soldiers. During the last two or three centuries the friends of God should have built a better social order because they were endowed with every tool for the task—the power of truth, the breastplate of justice, the gospel of peace, the shield of faith, the helmet of salvation, and the sword of the spirit. But these friends of truth and justice were apathetic and complacent. They allowed a social order to grow and spread which made the life of the masses tragic and salvation difficult.

Christian charity has not been lacking through the centuries. Kindly men and women in every age have ministered to the needs of the poor, not realizing that they were charitably giving crutches to cripples while justice demanded that there should not be so many cripples. To help the victims of poverty and wretchedness is charity; to stop the causes of their misery is justice. Many have pursued the beautiful virtue of charity, but justice—stern, lofty, and uncompromising—had no suitors.

Pope Pius XII has said that the great misery of the social order is that it is not deeply Christian nor really human and that the reorganization of the social order requires the efforts of all. In the presence of crisis and tragedy many Christians have been complacent. The damage has been done. We have a world to reconstruct. It is a time for high heroism and deep devotion, a time for *study* and *work*. To borrow again from the editorial, because it is so completely to the point:

. . . the essential purpose of Christianity is not to bring a new culture to the world, not even a new Christian culture. The function of the religion of redemption and transfiguration is rather to heal the wounds and infirmities of men and to put men in the way of obtaining eternal life. Since, however, man is essentially a personal entity which comprises a body and since being is a coherent system built up of various levels, a system created by God, ordered by Him and carried by Him, the work of healing, though it must begin in the soul, cannot end there; the world also needs healing and transfiguration and is capable of being thus healed and transfigured.

This change in the world is no automatic consequence of the conversion of the individual. It is not an emanation manifesting itself "somehow or other" out of the Christian spirit. It is a matter of *work.* . . .

Only the courage to hold our own faith will enable us to break free from our adherence to superannuated ideas, will enable us to think ahead for the future, will give us the daring to "experiment forward," to engage in that experiment in which, repeating itself in a thousand instances, the Christian's responsibility before the world, which he is ultimately under obligation to display, will at length be realized.

This volume points the way to a better social order and the dawn of a brighter day.

Most Reverend ROBERT E. LUCEY, S.T.D.

Archbishop of San Antonio
February 13, 1953

Introduction

THE SOVEREIGN PONTIFFS have voiced their concern regarding the economic ills of society. In answer to their warning, some students of the social problem within the past few years have been focusing attention upon a suggested solution known as the Industry Council Plan. Increasing interest in the Plan has made apparent the need for information bearing upon it. It has seemed desirable, therefore, to help meet this need by grouping in a systematic way papal statements pertinent to the principles involved in the Plan.

The need for the study of the socio-economic problem is urgent. The situation is so grave that Pope Pius XI in a general reference to it likened it to the emergency created by a national crisis.

When our country is in danger, everything not strictly necessary, everything not bearing directly on the urgent matter of unified defense, takes second place. So we must act in today's crisis. Every other enterprise, however attractive and helpful, must yield before the vital need of protecting the very foundation of the Faith and of Christian civilization. [DIVINI REDEMPTORIS, 62].

Because of today's crisis in our economic society the Sovereign Pontiffs have urged reform based on socio-ethical principles in keeping with the Divine and natural law. The Popes have not officially endorsed any specific plan; but, leaving concrete solutions to students of the

problem, have supplied the norms or principles which
must underlie any effective reform in the direction of economic co-operation.

The Industry Council Plan is an effort toward such a
reform in contemporary society. It is still in the formative
and controversial stage, and students in the field are not
in complete agreement on dynamic problems involved.
The present work does not attempt a solution of these
unsolved questions. Rather it offers papal statements bearing on the underlying principles of a workable socio-
economic system. The statements are arranged in a pattern of thought which may make the compilation useful
as a handbook for those desiring quotations bearing upon
these basic principles. It can serve also as a guide to classes
and other groups interested not only in the Industry
Council Plan, but also in the social question in general
and the principles which pertain to it.

Because of the many sources cited, abbreviated forms
of some of the titles are used; the key to these will be
found on pages 192 ff. The titles of encyclicals are indicated in brackets to distinguish them from other pronouncements. Since the writings of Pope Pius XII may
not be easily accessible to many readers, special effort
has been made to present pertinent statements from his
pen up to the time of the publication of this work.

The study is divided into three parts answering three
large questions: 1. *What Is the Industry Council Plan and
Why Is It Needed?* 2. *What Are the Principles Which
Apply Specifically to the Industry Council Plan?* 3. *What
Social Principles Are Indirectly Related to the Industry
Council Plan?*

It is well to observe that such papal expressions as "corporation," "professional organization," "industries and professions," and "vocational order" are similar to the term "Industry Council Plan," the expression commonly used by a number of American students of the problem.

The original manuscript was submitted to approximately forty authorities in the field of Catholic social teaching, and revisions have been made in accordance with their suggestions. The authors thank all those who generously gave assistance in evaluation and suggestion, particularly Reverend Richard Arès, S.J.; Reverend W. Norris Clarke, S.J.; Sister Mary Claudia, I.H.M.; Reverend Francis Corley, S.J.; Reverend John F. Cronin, S.S.; Reverend Mortimer Gavin, S.J.; Reverend George Higgins; the late Reverend Joseph Husslein, S.J.; Reverend Benjamin Masse, S.J.; Reverend Raymond Miller, C.Ss.R.; Reverend Raymond McGowan; Reverend Laurence McHattie, S.J.; Franz Mueller; Reverend Joseph Munier; Thomas Neill; Reverend Joseph Schuyler, S.J.; Reverend William J. Smith, S.J.; and Reverend Harold Trehey. Gratitude is expressed also to those who aided in the preparation of the manuscript for publication. The authors, however, take full responsibility for the contents as they appear in final form. They hope that this book may make some contribution to the emergence of a better social order, through a clearer understanding and appreciation of the meaning and objectives of the Industry Council Plan.

M.L.E.
G.J.S.

March 27, 1953

Part One

The Industry Council Plan

Chapter I

What Is the Industry Council Plan?

THE INDUSTRY COUNCIL PLAN is a proposed system of social and economic organization which would be functional, democratic, legally recognized but not government controlled, and balanced to achieve the recognition of both individual rights and the general welfare.

Basic in the Industry Council Plan are the councils which would be set up for each industry, profession, and agricultural group on the local, regional, national, and international levels. In some fields of production or service, local councils would not be necessary; in others, regional councils perhaps could be dispensed with. Besides these councils, there would also be inter-industry councils at the local, regional, national, and international levels to provide discussion and action agencies to harmonize the interests of all the industries, professions, and agricultural groups at specific levels.

Membership on a council would be determined by democratic elections, the voters being all individuals (or their delegates) whose interests are the concern of a council. Thus, a local industrial council would be composed of an equal number of representatives of the workers and an equal number of representatives of employers in a given industry, together with one or more representatives of the public. The latter could either be elected by the other members of the council, or, if the council so desired, be appointed by an appropriate unit of government. Again, a regional council would be composed of delegates of all local councils in that industry in that region; and the national inter-industry council would be made up of regional delegates. The national council would not be a political congress, but would have advisory powers and would make socio-economic legislative recommendations to the Congress.

Decisions approved by the councils would be binding on all workers and employers and would become part of the law of the land, to be enforced by government if self-enforcement failed. While direct setting of economic controls would not be a function of the councils at any level, their decisions would indirectly lead to the just price, the living wage, fair competition and so on, since they would create a climate of opinion favorable to the general welfare. Another function of government would be to restrain any industrial, professional, or agricultural council which made decisions contrary to the general welfare. While each industry, profession, and agricultural group would have its own commissions to handle disputes, appeals from these bodies could be taken to the federal or state courts.

Since the Industry Council Plan is democratic from local to international levels and since it follows the principle that lesser groups should perform the functions within their competence and not delegate these to larger groups, it is neither socialistic, fascistic, nor totalitarian. Private ownership and the rights of workers to a living wage and of employers to a fair profit would be maintained if the Plan were adopted. An extension of private ownership would be promoted while competition would be preserved as an essential part of the industrial process. The main changes from our present system would be that the limitations of competition sometimes demanded by the general welfare would be imposed by the industrial family itself rather than by government; labor-management hostility would be reduced; and all—workers, employers, professional people, farmers, consumers, and government—would co-operate in an economy designed to protect the rights, utilize most effectively the potentialities, and stimulate the performance of duties of each individual and group.

Those who favor the Industry Council Plan have no illusions about the possibility of putting it into practice without a great change in present social and individual thinking and practice. Neither do they expect that any master blueprint can be submitted to the nation for immediate adoption. But they do believe that certain portions of the Plan can be adopted gradually and that many of the details should be kept flexible until sufficient discussion, thought, and practice have demonstrated the superiority of one or the other detail in the organization. And they are convinced that if men of good will intelligently study the Plan they will see in it a system that is eminently adapted to the nature of man, to a recognition of individual rights, and to a realization of the general welfare (Statement approved July 15, 1950, by the Industry Council Plan Committee of the American Catholic Sociological Society).

SUGGESTED ORGANIZATION PLAN
FOR ONE INDUSTRY

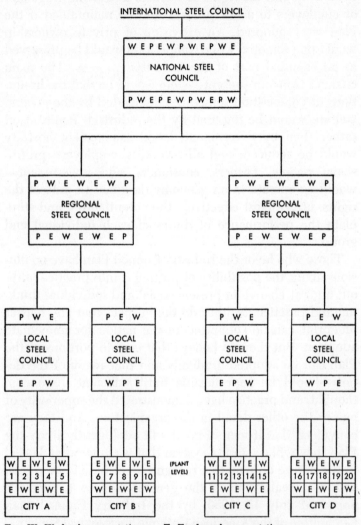

Key: W. Workers' representatives   E. Employers' representatives
P. Public representatives. At the lower levels, representatives of the public may or may not be included, depending on the circumstances. Where included, they may be appointed by the appropriate unit of government, or elected by the other members of the council.

SUGGESTED ORGANIZATION PLAN
FOR INTER-INDUSTRY COUNCILS

INTERNATIONAL INTER-INDUSTRY COUNCIL

NATIONAL INTER-INDUSTRY COUNCIL

Agriculture, Forestry, Fishing	Mining	Construction	Transportation and Communication	Trade	Finance, Insurance, Real Estate	Manufacturing	Business Services	Personal Services	Amusement and Recreation	Professions	Government Service
E P W	P W E	W E P	E P W	P W E	W E P	E P W	P W E	W E P	E P W	P W E	W E P

REGIONAL INTER-INDUSTRY COUNCILS

Agr. & For.	Mining	Construction	Trans. & Comm.	Trade	Fin., Ins., R.E.	Manufacturing	Busin. Service	Person. Serv.	Amusement	Professions	Govt. Service
P E W	E W P	W P E	P E W	E W P	W P E	P E W	E W P	W P E	P E W	E W P	W P E

Agr. & For.	Mining	Construction	Trans. & Comm.	Trade	Fin., Ins., R.E.	Manufacturing	Busin. Service	Person. Serv.	Amusement	Professions	Govt. Service
P E W	E W P	W P E	P E W	E W P	W P E	P E W	E W P	W P E	P E W	E W P	W P E

LOCAL INTER-INDUSTRY COUNCILS

Agr. & For.	Mining	Construction	Trans. & Com.	Trade	Fin., Ins., RE	Manufactur'g	Busin. Service	Person. Serv.	Amusement	Professions	Govt. Serv.
P E W	E W P	W P E	P E W	E W P	W P E	P E W	E W P	W P E	P E W	E W P	W P E

Agr. & For.	Mining	Construction	Trans. & Com.	Trade	Fin., Ins., RE	Manufactur'g	Busin. Serv.	Person. Serv.	Amusement	Professions	Govt. Serv.
P E W	E W P	W P E	P E W	E W P	W P E	P E W	E W P	W P E	P E W	E W P	W P E

Key: W. Workers' representatives   E. Employers' representatives
P. Public representatives. They may be appointed by the appropriate unit of government, or elected by the other members of the council.
Note: Grouping of occupations has no particular significance.

Chapter II

Why Is the Industry Council Plan Needed?

ITS NECESSITY

Abuses in Present Economic System. The Popes who have urged a reorganization of society preface their recommendations with an indictment of the abuses in the present economic system. Terms of uncompromising condemnation of the injustice existing in this system take such forms as "amoral liberalism" [DIVINI REDEMPTORIS, 32];* "greed for gain" (Action, 645); "false ideas" [QUADRAGESIMO ANNO, 54]; "galling yoke" [QUADRAGESIMO ANNO, 4]; "violation of justice" [QUADRAGESIMO ANNO, 4]; "idols of Liberalism" [QUADRAGESIMO ANNO, 14]; "worst of injustices and frauds" [QUADRAGESIMO ANNO, 132]; "enormous evils" [QUADRAGESIMO ANNO, 133]; "most sordid license" [QUADRAGESIMO ANNO, 132]; "despotic economic domination" [QUADRAGESIMO ANNO, 105]; "tragically hard, inexorable, and cruel" [QUADRAGESIMO ANNO, 109]; "grave evils" [QUADRAGESIMO ANNO, 109]; "the State . . . is become a slave, surrendered and delivered to the passions and greed

* See key, infra pp. 192 ff., for identification of sources.

of men" [QUADRAGESIMO ANNO, 109]; "[results in] accursed internationalism of finance or international imperialism" [QUADRAGESIMO ANNO, 109]; "vices" [QUADRAGESIMO ANNO, 109]; "savagery of greedy men" [RERUM NOVARUM, 59]; "devouring usury" [RERUM NOVARUM, 6]; "a yoke almost of slavery" [RERUM NOVARUM, 6]. Pius XI concludes, "And so . . . having surveyed the present economic system, We have found it laboring under the gravest of evils" [QUADRAGESIMO ANNO, 128].

Pope Pius XII also observes defects in the present system:

. . . one deplores the defects and clashes in human relations, resulting from the labor structure in the world of industrial capitalism. Complaint is made, in effect, that labor has, as it were, "lost its soul"; that is to say, the personal and social sense of human living. Complaint is made that labor, oppressed on all sides by a complexity of organizations, sees this human life transformed into a giant automaton, of which men are only the unconscious cogs. Complaint is made that technology, "standardizing" every move, works to the detriment of the individuality and personality of the worker (Rural Problems, 8).

The above comprises only a limited sampling of the stern language used in denouncing a perversion of the plan of Divine Providence in the use of creatures, both of the human and of the lower orders. The Holy Father writes this indictment:

In the social field the counterfeiting of God's plan has gone to its very roots by deforming the Divine image of man. Instead of his real created nature with origin and destiny in God, there has been substituted the false notion of a man whose conscience is a law unto himself, who is his own legislator brooking no control, who has no responsibility towards his fellows and society, with no destiny beyond the earth and no other purpose than the enjoyment of finite goods, with no rule of life except that of the *fait accompli* and the unbridled satisfaction of his desires.

As an outgrowth of this notion, which came to wield increasing power over a long period of years because of its most varied applications in public and private life, was that narrowly individualistic order which today is in serious crisis almost everywhere. But the more recent innovators have provided no better results. Starting from the same mistaken premises and taking the downward path in another direction, they have led to no less disastrous consequences, including the complete overthrow of the Divine order, contempt for the dignity of the human person, the denial of the most sacred and fundamental freedoms, the domination of a single class over the others, the enslavement of all persons and property in a totalitarian state, and to legalized violence and to militant atheism (Christmas 1949, 184).

Necessity for Reorganization. Progressing from a condemnation of the abuses in our present economy, the Popes show the necessity of a reorganization of society. The term "reorganization" is carefully chosen by commentators to indicate that a more correct order had existed in former times, notably the order maintained by the medieval guilds in the golden era of their existence. While the Pope does not advocate a return to these guilds, he does call attention to their success in building a society which met "the requirements of right reason."

The beneficent achievements of the guilds of artisans among our ancestors have long been well known. Truly, they yielded noteworthy advantages not only to artisans, but, as many monuments bear witness, brought glory and progress to the arts themselves. In our present age of greater culture, with its new customs and ways of living, and with the increased number of things required by daily life, it is most clearly necessary that workers' associations be adapted to meet the present need [RERUM NOVARUM, 69].

For there was a social order once which, although indeed not perfect or in all respects ideal, nevertheless, met in a certain measure the requirements of right reason, considering the conditions and needs of the time [QUADRAGESIMO ANNO, 97].

In seeming to anticipate the objections of defeatists who so often say that the plan is a beautiful ideal, but that it is necessary to be realistic, Pope Pius XI notes: "There were some also who stood, indeed, in awe at its splendor, but regarded it as a kind of imaginary ideal of perfection more desirable than attainable" [QUADRAGESIMO ANNO, 14]. The Pope continues:

If that order has long since perished, that surely did not happen because the order could not have accommodated itself to changed conditions and needs by development and by a certain expansion, but rather because men, hardened by too much love of self, refused to open the order to the increasing masses as they should have done, or because, deceived by allurements of a false freedom and other errors, they became impatient of every authority and sought to reject every form of control [QUADRAGESIMO ANNO, 97].

The reorganization called for does not imply an overturn of our economic system, but rather a reform "according to the norms of right order" building, by an evolutionary process, upon the existing system.

. . . the Encyclical of Our Predecessor of happy memory [Leo XIII] had in view chiefly that economic system, wherein, generally, some provide capital while others provide labor for a joint economic activity. And in a happy phrase he described it thus: "Neither capital can do without labor, nor labor without capital."

With all his energy Leo XIII sought to adjust this economic system according to the norms of right order; hence, it is evident that this system is not to be condemned in itself. And surely it is not of its own nature vicious. But it does violate right order when capital hires workers, that is, the non-owning working class, with a view to and under such terms that it directs business and even the whole economic system according to its own will and advantage, scorning the human dignity of the workers, the social character of economic activity and social justice itself, and the common good [QUADRAGESIMO ANNO, 100-101].

PAPAL INSISTENCE ON REFORM

Pope Pius XI, when speaking of the program set forth in RERUM NOVARUM which called for a truly Christian society, disproves the charge of impracticality.

All these benefits of Leo's Encyclical . . . which We have outlined rather than fully described, are so numerous and of such import as to show plainly that this immortal document does not exhibit a merely fanciful, even if beautiful, ideal of human society. Rather did Our Predecessor draw from the Gospel and, therefore, from an ever-living and life-giving fountain, teachings capable of greatly mitigating, if not immediately terminating that deadly internal struggle which is rending the family of mankind. The rich fruits which the Church of Christ and the whole human race have, by God's favor, reaped therefrom unto salvation prove that some of this good seed, so lavishly sown forty years ago, fell on good ground. On the basis of the long period of experience, it cannot be rash to say that Leo's Encyclical has proved itself the *Magna Charta* upon which all Christian activity in the social field ought to be based, as on a foundation [QUADRA-GESIMO ANNO, 39].

He then presents a dilemma of condemnation for those who reject it.

And those who would seem to hold in little esteem this Papal Encyclical and its commemoration either blaspheme what they know not, or understand nothing of what they are only superficially acquainted with, or if they do understand convict themselves formally of injustice and ingratitude [QUAD-RAGESIMO ANNO, 39].

Evidently the Pope had in mind a general reorganization of society in all its phases—the family, industrial relations, the State, international relations. Christian principles apply to all these fields; the purpose of this work is to apply them to industrial relations and to the "Industry Council Plan."

The redemption of the non-owning workers—this is the goal that Our Predecessor declared must necessarily be sought. And the point is the more emphatically to be asserted and more insistently repeated because the commands of the Pontiff, salutary as they are, have not infrequently been consigned to oblivion either because they were deliberately suppressed by silence or thought impracticable although they both can and ought to be put into effect. And these commands have not lost their force and wisdom for our time because that "pauperism" which Leo XIII beheld in all its horror is less widespread [QUADRAGESIMO ANNO, 59].

. . . it is of the utmost importance to foster in all classes of society an intensive program of social education adapted to the varying degrees of intellectual culture. It is necessary with all care and diligence to procure the widest possible diffusion of the teachings of the Church, even among the working classes. The minds of men must be illuminated with the sure light of Catholic teaching, and their wills must be drawn to follow and apply it as the norm of right living in the conscientious fulfillment of their manifold social duties. Thus they will oppose that incoherence and discontinuity in Christian life which We have many times lamented [DIVINI REDEMPTORIS, 55].

Pope Pius XII takes a no less insistent stand:

. . . the teaching and exhortations of the Roman Pontiffs, especially in the course of recent decades, dealing with the conduct of Christians toward the neighbor, society, and the State—all this serves to proclaim the believer's duty to take his share, generously, courageously, and according to his station and capacity, in questions that a tormented and agitated world has to solve in the field of social justice, no less than on the international plane of law and peace.

A convinced Christian cannot confine himself within an easy and egotistical "isolationism," when he witnesses the needs and the misery of his brothers; when pleas for help come to him from these in economic distress; when he knows the aspirations of the working classes for more normal and just conditions of life; when he is aware of the abuses of an economic system which puts money above social obligations; when he is not ignorant of the aberrations of an intransigent nationalism which denies or spurns the common bonds linking the separate nations together, and imposing on each one of them many and varied duties toward the great family of nations (Christmas 1948, 18).

It is not a question today of merely distributing the products of the social economy more equitably in closer correspondence with the labor and the needs of individuals. Important as this requirement may be, still under present conditions, especially in view of the enormous destruction and fluctuation caused by the war, every social reform is strictly bound up with the question of a prudent organization of production.

The relations between agriculture and industry within the single national economies, and of those latter with the economy of other nations, the manner and extent that each nation is to share in the world market—all these difficult problems present themselves today afresh and under aspects different from those of previous times. Upon their rational solution depends the productivity of the several nations, and consequently the welfare of individuals as well; for it is clear that there can never be sufficient distribution where there is not sufficient production (Name Day 1948, 485).

. . . the very idea of Christianity demands the creation of a more exact judicial order. This is especially true of that group of formidable problems which refer to the setting up of an economic and social order more in keeping with the eternal law of God and with the dignity of man. In it Christian thought insists, as a substantial element, on the raising of the proletariat; the achievement of this in a resolute and generous manner appears to every true follower of Christ not only as a step forward along the path of earthly progress, but also as the fulfillment of a moral obligation (Reconstruction 1944, 579).

That the problem, once with us, has been solved, Pope Pius XII denies in these words:

. . . it is not only the social status of workers, men and women, which calls for reconditioning and reform. The whole complex structure of society is in need of adjustment and improvement, thoroughly shaken as it is in its foundations.

But who is there who does not see that the labor question, because of the complexity and variety of the problems which it entails and the vast number of people it involves, is of such a kind and of such urgent importance as to merit closer, more watchful and more far-seeing attention?

.   .   .   .

That [improvement], however, should not lead any one to think, as We insisted in Our message of last Christmas, that all these questions are to be considered as solved (Italian Workers 1943, 2-3).

When consulted on the question of nationalization, Pope Pius XII writes M. Flory, President of Semaines Sociales de France, that the workable solution to the social problem is rather the "establishment of associations or corporate groups."

In Our judgment the establishment of associations or corporate groups in all the branches of the national economy would be much more conducive [than nationalization] both to the realization of the end which you pursue and at the same time to the greater success of the enterprises. At any rate, this was certainly true wherever, as it was up to this time, the concentration of enterprises and the disappearance of small independent producers were working only in favor of capital and not in favor of the public economy. There is no doubt, besides, that, in the present circumstances, the corporative form of social, and especially of economic, life is, in practice, favorable to the Christian doctrines regarding the person, the community, labor and private property (Semaines 1946, 2).

Papal Appeal to Clergy. The Popes address this special appeal to the Cardinals:

To you especially the invitation is addressed to collaborate without reserve in forming a public order which will realize, in the highest possible degree, a healthy economic life and social justice (Name Day 1947, 20).

To Priests:

Errors of both economic systems [Communism and excessive or exaggerated capitalism] and the harmful results deriving from them must persuade everyone, especially priests, to remain faithful to the social teaching of the Church, to spread the knowledge of it and, to the extent of their power, to reduce it to practical application (Menti Nostrae, 123).

Let our parish priests, therefore, while providing of course for the normal needs of the Faithful, dedicate the better part of their endeavors and their zeal to winning back the laboring masses to Christ and to His Church [DIVINI REDEMPTORIS, 62].

It is chiefly your duty, Venerable Brethren, and of your clergy, to search diligently for these lay apostles both of workers and of employers, to select them with prudence, and to train and instruct them properly. A difficult task, certainly, is thus imposed on priests, and to meet it, all who are growing up as the hope of the Church, must be duly prepared by an intensive study of the social question. Especially is it necessary that those whom you intend to assign in particular to this work should demonstrate that they are men possessed of the keenest sense of justice, who will resist with true manly courage the dishonest demands or the unjust acts of anyone, who will excel in the prudence and judgment which avoids every extreme, and above all, who will be deeply permeated by the charity of Christ, which alone has the power to subdue firmly but gently the hearts and wills of men to the laws of justice and equity. Upon this road so often tried by happy experience, there is no reason why we should hesitate to go forward with all speed [QUADRAGESIMO ANNO, 142].

To priests in a special way We recommend anew the oft-repeated counsel of Our Predecessor, Leo XIII, to go to the workingman. We make this advice Our own, and faithful to the teachings of Jesus Christ and His Church, We thus complete it: "Go to the workingman, especially where he is poor; and in general, go to the poor" [DIVINI REDEMPTORIS, 61].

Papal Appeal to Groups. To associations, such as labor unions and employer groups:

And may these free organizations, now flourishing and rejoicing in their salutary fruits, set before themselves the task of preparing the way, in conformity with the mind of Christian social teaching, for those larger and more important guilds, industries, and professions, which We mentioned before, and make every possible effort to bring them to realization [QUADRAGESIMO ANNO, 87].

We are thinking likewise of those associations of workmen, farmers, technicians, doctors, employers, students and others of like character, groups of men and women who live in the same cultural atmosphere and share the same way of life. Precisely these groups and organizations are destined to introduce into society that order which We have envisaged in Our Encyclical QUADRAGESIMO ANNO, and thus to spread in the vast and various fields of culture and labor the recognition of the Kingdom of Christ [DIVINI REDEMPTORIS, 68].

To agricultural workers:

It is, moreover, important that you should recognize the necessity for union with all the other professional or vocational groups that are supplying the various needs of the people, and thus signify your adherence to the principle of social peace (Farmer, 446).

Papal Appeal to All. To all faithful sons and daughters:

At the end of this war [World War II], which has upset all the activities of human life and has turned them into new channels, the problem of the future shaping of the social order will give rise to a fierce struggle between the various policies. In this struggle the Christian social idea has the arduous but noble mission of bringing forward and demonstrating theoretically and in practice to the followers of other schools, that in this field, so important for the peaceful development of relations between men, the postulates of true equity and the principles of Christianity can be united in close wedlock and bring forth security and prosperity for all those who can lay aside prejudice and passion and give ear to the teaching of truth. We are confident that our faithful sons and daughters of the Catholic world, as heralds of the Christian social idea, will contribute—even at the price of considerable sacrifices—to progress toward that social justice after which all true disciples of Christ must hunger and thirst (Reconstruction 1944, 582).

There are nations, of course, who can boast today of a productive capacity which, they point out, is constantly increasing from year to year. But if this productivity is attained as a result of unbridled competition and of an unprincipled expenditure of wealth, or by oppression and despotic exploitation of labor and the needs of individuals on the part of the State, it cannot be sound and natural, because social economy is an organizing of workers, and every worker is endowed with human dignity and freedom. The immoderate exploitation of genuine human values usually keeps step with that of nature's treasures, especially of the land, and leads sooner or later to decadence.

Only on the principles of Christianity and in accord with its spirit can the social reforms, called for imperatively by the necessities and aspirations of our times, be carried out. They demand from some the spirit of renunciation and sacrifice, from others the sense of responsibility and endurance, from everybody hard and strenuous work.

Wherefore, We turn to the Catholics of the whole world, exhorting them not to be satisfied with good intentions and fine projects but to proceed courageously to put them into practice. Neither should they hesitate to join forces with those who, remaining outside their ranks, are none the less in agreement with the social teaching of the Catholic Church and are disposed to follow the road that she has marked out, which is not the road of violent revolution but of experience, that has stood the test, and of energetic resolution (Name Day 1948, 485-486).

Again, in addressing the financiers who attended the Congress of International Exchange in 1948, Pope Pius XII said:

We limit ourselves to stressing certain fundamental concepts:

1. *Economic life means social life.* The essential scope of the former—to which individuals are equally bound to help in the different spheres of their activity—is to assure in a stable manner for all members of society the material conditions required for the development of cultural and spiritual life. But satisfactory results are not possible apart from an external order and social norms which aim at lasting achievement of this objective. An appeal to an automatic and magic law is a mirage, no less vain in the economic order than in any other sphere of human activity (Exchange, 422).

Those Who Ignore Papal Appeal. Refusal to co-operate is commented on in serious tones:

What is to be thought of the action of those Catholic employers who in one place succeeded in preventing the reading of Our Encyclical QUADRAGESIMO ANNO in their local churches? Or of those Catholic industrialists who even to this day have shown themselves hostile to a labor movement that We Ourselves recommended [DIVINI REDEMPTORIS, 50]?

. . . the commands of the Pontiff, salutary as they are, have not infrequently been consigned to oblivion either because they were deliberately suppressed by silence or thought impracticable although they both can and ought to be put into effect. And these commands have not lost their force and wisdom for our time because that "pauperism" which Leo XIII beheld in all its horror is less widespread [QUADRAGESIMO ANNO, 59].

At another time Pope Pius XI points up the inconsistency of those who ignore papal insistence.

For there are very many who profess Catholic teaching concerning social authority and the due regard to be paid to it, the rights of property, the rights and duties of laborers on the land or in industry . . . relations between capital and labor. . . . But in their words, writings, and in the whole tenor of their lives they behave as if the teaching and precepts so often promulgated by Supreme Pontiffs, by Leo XIII in special manner, by Pius X and Benedict XV, had lost their native strength and authority or were completely obsolete.

In this there can be recognized a certain kind of modernism in morals, in matters touching authority and the social order, the which, along with modernism in dogma, We specifically condemn [UBI ARCANO DEI, pp. 308-309].

Pope Pius XII identifies the teaching authority exercised by the Popes in the encyclicals in answer to those who regard them only as "advice."

Do not let die in your midst and fade away the insistent call of the social Encyclical, that voice which indicates to the Faithful in the supernatural regeneration of mankind the moral obligation to co-operate in the arrangement of society and especially of economic life, exhorting those who share in this life to action no less than the estate itself (Pentecost, 14).

Pope Pius XII summarizes this insistence in his 1949 address to the Belgian workers in which he again calls for the "drafting of a public law covering economic life":

The strength of an organization, no matter how powerful one may consider it to be, is not of itself an element of order. Recent and current history gives continuously tragic proof. Whoever has eyes to see can easily convince himself of this. Today, as yesterday, in the future as in the past, a firm and solid position can be built only on the foundations laid by nature, and in reality by the Creator, as the basis of the sole genuine stability.

This is why We never tire of recommending the immediate drafting of a public law covering economic life and all society, according to the organization of industries and professions. Here is why We also never tire of recommending an increase in the number of owners of private property, of medium and of small industries (Belgian Workers, 61).

Pope Pius XII when addressing the Catholic Congress on Rural Problems in July, 1951, voiced the challenge and opportunity for reform.

Today, men have the opportunity of deciding whether they will continue to follow a policy of one-sided and shortsighted "Quest of profit," or rather will begin to look toward the totality of the social economy, which is its objective end (Rural Problems, 8).

Respect for human rights and the promotion of the general welfare have suffered from abuses in the present socio-economic system. Reform is urgently called for by the Popes—a reform based on reason and on principles flowing from the nature of man and society. The Industry Council Plan seeks to build such an order established on the principles which are discussed by the Sovereign Pontiffs in the following chapters. This reform does not imply a revolution or overthrow of the present system but rather an evolution toward an ordered, organic society.

Part Two

Specific Principles Involved
in the
Industry Council Plan

Chapter III

Organic Structure

THE POPES have not advocated any detailed blueprint of economic organization, but have set down the principles which should govern such a society. These principles are the foundation upon which the Industry Council Plan is conceived. Still in the formative stage, the details of the Plan are the subject of differing opinions. However, agreement exists regarding the fundamental principles basic to the Plan. These principles, as classified in *Foundations of a Modern Guild System* by Harold Trehey and published by Catholic University of America Press in 1940, include organic structure, subsidiarity, liberty, self-government, graded structure, public-legal status, general welfare, and limited State intervention.

Present Society. The first principle is that of organic structure, the reconstitution of which is necessary for social order. The Holy Father sees the atomization of society brought about by the destruction of organic unity which had flourished in earlier times. Now our present order— or lack of it—is made up "only of individuals and the State."

When we speak of the reform of institutions, the State comes chiefly to mind, not as if universal well-being were to be expected from its activity, but because things have come to such a pass through the evil of what we have termed "individualism," that, following upon the overthrow and near extinction of that rich social life which was once highly developed through associations of various kinds, there remain virtually only individuals and the State. This is to the great harm of the State itself; for, with a structure of social governance lost, and with the taking over of all the burdens which the wrecked associations once bore, the State has been overwhelmed and rushed by almost infinite tasks and duties [QUADRAGESIMO ANNO, 78].

The vacuum created by the absence of unity thrust an added burden on the State and divided men on the "labor market":

Nevertheless, as the situation now stands, hiring and offering for hire in the so-called labor market separate men into two divisions, as into battle lines, and the contest between these divisions turns the labor market itself almost into a battlefield where, face to face, the opposing lines struggle bitterly. Everyone understands that this grave evil which is plunging all human society to destruction must be remedied as soon as possible [QUADRAGESIMO ANNO, 83].

This is a far cry from the true nature of man and society. Pope Leo XIII puts it no less baldly when he reminds us that "it is shameful and inhuman, however, to use men as things for gain and to put no more value on them than what they are worth in muscle and energy" [RERUM NOVARUM, 31], and "to take for granted that the one class of society is of itself hostile to the other, as if nature had set rich and poor against each other to fight fiercely in implacable war" [RERUM NOVARUM, 28].

In the first place must be put that "class warfare" which has penetrated among the nations like a deadly infection, poisoning work, the arts, commerce, everything, in fact, that tends to private and public well-being. And the evil is made worse by the increasing lust for material goods on the one side, tenacity in holding them on the other, on both sides desire for possession and power. Thence come frequent strikes and lock-outs, public disturbance and repression, damage and discontent for all [UBI ARCANO DEI, 298].

There can be no natural, organic unity among those engaged in production so long as quantitative utilitarianism—the consideration of maximum profitability—is the sole norm which determines the location of plants and the distribution of work, so long as the concept of "class" artificially divides men in Society, and there no longer exists a spirit of co-operation within occupational groups (World Federalism, 394).

Those who insist that class strife is unavoidable are refuted by Pope Pius XII. He states, rather, that employers and workers "are co-operators in a common task."

We have just made reference to the preoccupations of those who are engaged in industrial production. Mistaken and disastrous in its consequences is the prejudice, alas! too widely held, which sees in these problems an irreducible clash of rival interests. The opposition is only apparent. In the economic domain management and labor are linked in a community of action and interest. To disregard this mutual bond, to strive to break it, can only betray a pretention to blind and preposterous despotism. Employers and workers are not implacable adversaries. They are co-operators in a common task. They eat, so to speak, at the same table, seeing that they must live, in the last analysis, from the gross or net profits of the national economy. Each receives his income, and in this regard their mutual relations do not in any way imply that one is at the service of the other.

To receive one's wage is a prerogative of the personal dignity of anyone who makes his productive contribution in one form or another, as employer or laborer, towards the output of the nation's economy. In the accounting of private industry salary-totals may be listed under costs to the employer. But in the national economy there is only one type of costs, which consists in the national resources utilized with a view to national production, and which must, in consequence, be constantly replenished.

From this it follows that both parties are interested in seeing to it that the costs of national production are in proportion to its output. But since the interest is common, why should it not manifest itself in a common outward expression? Why should it not be allowable to assign to the workers just share of responsibility in the establishment and development of the national economy? Especially today when the scarcity of capital and the difficulty of international exchange are paralyzing the free flow of expenditure on national production? The recent attempts at socialization have only served to make this painful reality more clearly evident. It is a fact. Neither has it been created by the bad will of some, nor can the good will of others succeed in eliminating it. This being true, why not come to a decision now, while there is yet time, in full awareness of the common responsibility, so as to insure one group against unjust suspicions and the other against illusions which would become before long a social peril (Employers, 445-446)?

Therefore:

You will be able to fulfill these duties only with a great love. Fight hatred, hatred between nations as well as class hatred. Hatred can only destroy. Love builds. Against the forces of patience and of love that spring from faith in Christ and love for Him, irreligiousness, brutal egoism and class hatred must finally be shattered (Catholic Action, 54).

The Church never ceases to labor so that the apparent conflict between capital and labor, between the employer and the worker, be transformed into a higher unity, which means to say, into that organic co-operation of both parties which is indicated by their very nature and which consists in the collaboration of both according to their activity in the economic sector and the professions (Problem, 703).

True Nature of Organic Structure. *a. Unity.* Individuals are not "isolated units, like grains of sand, but united by the very force of their nature and by their internal destiny, into an organic, harmonious mutual relationship which varies with the changing of times" [SUMMI PONTIFICATUS, 37].

We are bound together by the "law of human solidarity and charity which is dictated and imposed by our common origin and by the equality of rational nature in all men, to whatever people they belong, and by the redeeming Sacrifice offered by Jesus Christ on the Altar of the Cross to His Heavenly Father on behalf of sinful mankind" [SUMMI PONTIFICATUS, 30].

. . . just as in the human body the different members harmonize with one another, whence arises that disposition of parts and proportion in the human figure rightly called symmetry, so likewise nature has commanded in the case of the State that the two classes mentioned should agree harmoniously and should properly form equally balanced counterparts to each other. Each needs the other completely: neither capital can do without labor, nor labor without capital. Concord begets beauty and order in things. Conversely, from perpetual strife

there must arise disorder accompanied by bestial cruelty. But
for putting an end to conflict and for cutting away its very
roots, there is wondrous and multiple power in Christian
institutions [RERUM NOVARUM, 28].

Indeed:

If the members of the body social are, as was said, recon-
stituted, and if the directing principle of economic-social life
is restored, it will be possible to say in a certain sense even of
this body what the Apostle says of the mystical body of Christ:
"The whole body (being closely joined and knit together
through every joint of the system according to the functioning
in due measure of each single part) derives its increase to the
building up of itself in love" (Eph. 4:16) [QUADRAGESIMO
ANNO, 90].

b. Function. The unity to be achieved in organic structure is to be brought about by organization based on the
function performed by members of the social body. Just as
the physical body is characterized by autonomy and diversity of function, so should the social body be characterized by a certain autonomy and diversity of function. This
very function provides the bond of union, another essential
in the Industry Council Plan.

But complete cure will not come until this opposition has been
abolished and well-ordered members of the social body—Industries and Professions—are constituted in which men may
have their place, not according to the position each has in the
labor market but according to the respective social functions
which each performs. For under nature's guidance it comes to
pass that just as those who are joined together by nearness of
habitation establish towns, so those who follow the same industry or profession—whether in the economic or other field

—form guilds or associations, so that many are wont to consider these self-governing organizations, if not essential, at least natural to civil society.

Because order, as St. Thomas well explains, is unity arising from the harmonious arrangement of many objects, a true, genuine social order demands that the various members of a society be united together by some strong bond. This unifying force is present not only in the producing of goods or the rendering of services—in which the employers and employees of an identical Industry or Profession collaborate jointly—but also in that common good, to achieve which all Industries and Professions together ought, each to the best of its ability, to co-operate amicably. And this unity will be the stronger and more effective, the more faithfully individuals and the Industries and Professions themselves strive to do their work and excel in it [QUADRAGESIMO ANNO, 83-84].

The same is true of Our position with respect to professional or "corporative" organization, which has also been made the object of sundry and conflicting interpretations in public disputes—in some cases, perhaps, because of misunderstanding. Here also Our position is identically that of the Encyclical QUADRAGESIMO ANNO, safely above all reproach of interference in the purely political affairs of our times. But this social doctrine may well provide our generation with a highly pertinent object lesson and orientation.

Over and above the distinction between employer and employe, which threatens more seriously every day to become a pitiless separation, there is human labor itself: the work to be done, the job to which every man contributes something vital and personal, with a view to supplying society with goods and services adequate to its needs. It lies in the very nature of labor, understood in this sense, to draw men together in a genuine and intimate union, and to restore form and structure to a society which has become shapeless and unstable. This in turn would infuse new life into the relations between society and the State.

By contrast, those who would make of society and State a mere conglomeration of laboring-men, disregard the fundamental nature of labor and civil society. Labor is emptied of its real meaning and denied its inward unifying power. In the last analysis, these people are not here planning to organize men—laborers considered as men—but to heap up a gigantic sum of incomes in the form of salaries or wages. The danger that economic forces may control the State, to the serious detriment of the general welfare, is every bit as serious in this instance, as when the State is subject to the dominating influence of capital (Semaines 1947, 681-682).

Responsibility of All for Co-operation. Responsibility toward this social body rests on the individuals, the employers, the unions and the workers, demanding of all a spirit of co-operation.

Its [social doctrine of the Church] realization requires of all participants in the process a discretion born of insight and foresight, a strong dose of good sense and good will. It demands of them especially a radical reaction against the temptation to seek each one's own advantage at the expense of the other partners—whatever be the nature and form of their participation—and to the detriment of the common welfare. It calls finally for unselfishness of a sort which can only be instilled by an authentic Christian virtue, sustained and aided by the grace of God (Employers, 447-448).

The Church likewise counsels all to use whatever contributes toward making relations between employer and workers more human, more Christian, and more conducive to mutual confidence. The class struggle can never be a social end. The discussions between employers and workers must have as their main aim peace and collaboration (Spanish Employers and Workers, 707).

Indeed, were they [labor unions] to aim at exclusive control in the State and society; should they want to have the workman completely in their power; if they stifled the stern voice of justice and the honest desire to collaborate with the other social classes, they would prove false to the expectations and the hopes placed in them by every decent, conscientious workingman (Italian Workers 1948, 615).

Each social group has an important role to play in the transformation that the world is undergoing, and it is only too clear that the working class in matters that concern it is called today to assume responsibilities that it has never known in the past (Christian Workers, 509).

Why, then, does not this common uncertainty and doubt, arising from present circumstances, create a certain solidarity among the peoples in different countries? Is not the interest of the employer and the employed in this respect identical? Is it not true in every country that industrial and agricultural production are now more than ever linked together on account of the reciprocal influence they exert one upon the other . . . ?

Why should not this solidarity among all those peoples who are restless and in danger become for all the secure way leading to safety? Why should not this spirit of solidarity be the basis of the natural social order in its three essentials—the family, property, and the State—and make these elements collaborate in one organic whole that is adapted to present conditions? These present conditions are, after all, despite all their inherent difficulties, a gift of God; why should they not conduce to the strengthening of the Christian spirit (Christmas 1950, 206)?

Finally, the Sovereign Pontiffs warn of the necessity of this organic structure:

For man's productive effort cannot yield its fruits unless a truly social and organic body exists, unless a social and juridical order watches over the exercise of work, unless the various occupations, being interdependent, co-operate with and mutually complete one another, and, what is still more important, unless mind, material things, and work combine and form as it were a single whole [QUADRAGESIMO ANNO, 69].

Pope Pius XII explains further:

Reason, enlightened by faith, assigns to individuals and to particular societies in the social organization a definite and exalted place. It knows, to mention only the most important, that the whole political and economic activity of the State is directed to the permanent realization of the common good. It is to create those external conditions which are needed for the mass of the citizens, to bring their natural virtues to maturity, to fulfill their office and develop fully their material, intellectual, and religious life—insofar as the family, on the one hand, and other associations to which nature has given precedence over the State, on the other hand, may be physically and morally insufficient for their needs—that God's redeeming will has not established another and universal society within the Church to direct the human individual and bring him to the attaining of his supernatural destiny. In a conception of society which is pervaded and sanctioned by religious thought, the influence of economics and of every other sphere of cultural activity represents a universal and most exalted center of activity, very rich in its variety and coherent in its harmony, in which men's intellectual equality and diversity of occupation come into their own and secure adequate expression.

When this is not so work is depreciated, and the worker is belittled (Christmas 1942, 6-7).

Pope Leo XIII shows this necessity to be rooted in nature.

Inadequacy of his own strength, learned from experience, impels and urges a man to enlist the help of others. Such is the teaching of Holy Scripture: "It is better therefore that two should be together, than one: for they have the advantage of their society. If one fall he shall be supported by the other; woe to him that is alone, for when he falleth he hath none to lift him up" (Eccles. 4: 9-10). And this also: "A brother that is helped by his brother, is like a strong city" (Prov. 18: 19). Just as man is drawn by this natural propensity into civil union and association, so also he seeks with his fellow citizens to form other societies, admittedly small and not perfect, but societies none the less [RERUM NOVARUM, 70].

In his 1945 address to the Italian Workers, Pope Pius XII again urges "a new organization of the productive forces":

It is now time to abandon empty phrases and to think along with QUADRAGESIMO ANNO toward a new organization of the productive forces of the people that is above distinction between employers and workers. Men should see and recognize that higher unity which joins together all those who collaborate in production; that is to say, in their union and solidarity, in the duty which both have to provide constantly for the common welfare and the needs of all the community.

May this solidarity extend to all branches of production, may it become the foundation of a better economic order, or a sound and just autonomy, and may it open the way for the working classes to acquire their part and responsibility in the conduct of the national economy!

In this way, thanks to this harmonious co-ordination and co-operation, to this more intimate union of labor with the other factors of economic life, the laborer will succeed in finding in his activity tranquil earning sufficient for his support and his family's, true satisfaction for his soul and a powerful incentive toward his improvement (Italian Workers 1945, 5, 22).

Chapter IV

Subsidiarity

Meaning and Function. The second principle on which the Industry Council Plan is based—subsidiarity—dictates that "a greater and higher association" should not do "what lesser and subordinate organizations can do." In identifying this principle and the grave importance of its observance Pope Pius XI says this:

As history abundantly proves, it is true that on account of changed conditions many things which were done by small associations in former times cannot be done now save by large associations. Still, that most weighty principle, which cannot be set aside or changed, remains fixed and unshaken in social philosophy: Just as it is gravely wrong to take from individuals what they can accomplish by their own initiative and industry and give it to the community, so also it is an injustice and at the same time a grave evil and disturbance of right order to assign to a greater and higher association what lesser and subordinate organizations can do. For every social activity ought of its very nature to furnish help to the members of the body social, and never destroy and absorb them [QUADRAGESIMO ANNO, 79].

Pope Pius XII underlines this thought when he maintains that "every social activity is of its nature subsidiary;

it must serve as a support to members of the social body and never destroy or absorb them. These are surely enlightened words, valid for social life in all its grades . . ." (Society, 196).

Again he warns against an extreme position in opposing laissez-faire.

On the other hand, it is clearly our bounden duty today, when the former propensity for the "hands-off" system of laissez-faire shows serious signs of weakening, to beware of plunging to the opposite extreme. In organizing production, we must guarantee full weight and directive influence to the principle, advanced time and again in the social teaching of the Church, according to which the activity and services of society must play a merely "subsidiary" role, aiding or supplementing the activity of the individual, the family, and the profession (Semaines 1947, 683).

Consequences flowing from the State's disregard of subsidiarity will harm public welfare by discouraging private initiative and responsibility.

To consider the State as something ultimate to which everything else should be subordinated and directed, cannot fail to harm the true and lasting prosperity of nations. This can happen either when unrestricted dominion comes to be conferred on the State as having a mandate from the nation, people, or even a social order, or when the State arrogates such dominion to itself as absolute master, despotically, without any mandate whatsoever. If, in fact, the State lays claim to and directs private enterprises, these, ruled as they are by delicate and complicated internal principles which guarantee and assure the realization of their special aims, may be damaged to the detriment of the public good, by being wrenched from their natural surroundings, that is, from responsible private action [SUMMI PONTIFICATUS, 55].

Position of the State. Pope Leo draws a fine line of distinction for State action, delimiting its area of action. "Let the State protect these lawfully associated bodies of citizens; let it not, however, interfere with their private concerns and order of life; for vital activity is set in motion by an inner principle, and it is very easily destroyed, as We know, by intrusion from without" [RERUM NOVARUM, 75]. Elsewhere he specifically mentions situations in which the State has the duty of acting:

It is vitally important to public as well as to private welfare that there be peace and good order; likewise, that the whole regime of family life be directed according to the ordinances of God and the principles of nature, that religion be observed and cultivated, that sound morals flourish in private and public life, that justice be kept sacred and that no one be wronged with impunity by another, and that strong citizens grow up, capable of supporting, and, if necessary, of protecting the State. Wherefore, if at any time disorder should threaten because of strikes or concerted stoppages of work, if the natural bonds of family life should be relaxed among the poor, if religion among the workers should be outraged by failure to provide sufficient opportunity for performing religious duties, if in factories danger should assail the integrity of morals through the mixing of the sexes or other pernicious incitements to sin, or if the employer class should oppress the working class with unjust burdens or should degrade them with conditions inimical to human personality or to human dignity, if health should be injured by immoderate work and such as is not suited to sex or age—in all these cases, the power and authority of the law, but of course within certain limits, manifestly ought to be employed. And these limits are determined by the same reason which demands the aid of the law, that is, the law ought not undertake more, nor ought it go farther, than the remedy of evils or the removal of danger requires [RERUM NOVARUM, 53].

Today, however, because we lack the organization provided for in the Industry Council Plan, the government is burdened with more than would be necessary in a well-ordered society.

Certainly today, in the inextricable confusion in which the world is tossing, the State finds itself compelled to take over an immense weight of duties and offices; but does not this abnormal state of affairs threaten gravely to compromise its essential force and the efficiency of its authority (Society, 200)?

Pope Pius XI indicates the proper role of the government in a well-ordered socio-economic system in which the principle of subsidiarity is duly observed.

The supreme authority of the State ought, therefore, to let subordinate groups handle matters and concerns of lesser importance, which would otherwise dissipate its efforts greatly. Thereby the State will more freely, powerfully, and effectively do all those things that belong to it alone because it alone can do them: directing, watching, urging, restraining, as occasion requires and necessity demands. Therefore, those in power should be sure that the more perfectly a graduated order is kept among the various associations, in observance of the principle of "subsidiary function," the stronger social authority and effectiveness will be and the happier and more prosperous the condition of the State [QUADRAGESIMO ANNO, 80].

These four functions of the State are developed more at length in Chapter X, infra, pp. 82 ff.

It is to be remembered that the application of the principles of subsidiarity and government action to the concrete situations in the American socio-economic scene still presents many problems which remain to be solved and constitute an area of controversy and difference of opinion.

Chapter V

Liberty

EVEN THOUGH the Popes have not stressed liberty in their discussions of reorganization (due in large part to their concern in correcting the excessive license of laissez-faire individualism), it is pertinent to include the principle here. It is true that the emphasis in the Industry Council Plan is on unity and the common good, but liberty is an integral part of the Plan as well and is related to the principle of subsidiarity and self-government. In a number of papal statements liberty is considered in relation to various situations, which statements are applicable also to the socio-economic sphere.

Championed by the Church. True liberty, the third principle, is necessary to the proper exercise of the duties and rights of man in relation to society. Therefore, "The Church has always most faithfully fostered civil liberty" [LIBERTAS PRAESTANTISSIMUM, 34]. "Nor is there any reason why anyone should accuse the Church of being wanting in gentleness of action or largeness of view, or of being opposed to real and lawful liberty" [IMMORTALE DEI, 36]. ". . . true human liberty . . . is the indispensable element of the social order, considered as the organism of peace" (Christmas 1951, 255). ". . . the Christian order, since its purpose is peace, is essentially an order of liberty. It is the co-operative effort of free men and peoples toward the progressive realization in all spheres of life of the ends which God has assigned to humanity" (Christmas 1951, 254). "Liberty is a power perfecting man, and hence should have truth and goodness for its object" [IMMORTALE DEI, 32].

Let them therefore realize how much they and they alone can really and efficaciously contribute to the work of reconstruction, and that it will never reach a happy conclusion if it is not based on right, on order and liberty—on liberty, we wish to emphasize, to reach out to what is true and good, liberty such as will be in harmony with the well-being of every people in particular and of the whole great family of peoples. Such liberty the Church has ever proclaimed, guarded, and defended (Peace, 452-453).

Opposed to License. This genuine liberty has been repudiated by those who want to remove restraint from their lives and to substitute for it a false liberty or license.

The Popes thus describe the character of this license, as opposed to genuine liberty, and note the evil consequences flowing from the reign of the former:

As against this picture of the democratic ideal of liberty and equality in a people's government by honest and farseeing men, what a spectacle is that of a democratic State left to the whims of the masses:

Liberty, from being a moral duty of the individual, becomes a tyrannous claim to give free reign to a man's impulses and appetites to the detriment of others.

Equality degenerates to a mechanical level, a colorless uniformity, the sense of true honor, of personal activity, or respect for tradition, of dignity—in a word all that gives life its worth —gradually fades away and disappears.

And the only survivors are, on the one hand, the victims deluded by the specious mirage of democracy, naïvely taken for the genuine spirit of democracy with its liberty and equality; and on the other the more or less numerous exploiters who have known how to use the power of money and of organization in order to secure a privileged position above the others, and have gained power.

The democratic State, whether it be monarchical or republican, should, like any other form of government, be entrusted with the power to command with real and effective authority (Christmas 1944, 69).

In the same way the Church cannot approve of that liberty which begets a contempt of the most sacred laws of God, and casts off the obedience due to lawful authority, for this is not liberty so much as license, and is most correctly styled by St. Augustine the "liberty of self-ruin," and by the apostle St. Peter the *cloak of malice* (I Peter 2:16). Indeed, since it is opposed to reason, it is a true slavery, for whosoever committeth sin is the slave of sin (John 8:34). On the other hand, that liberty is truly genuine, and to be sought after, which in regard to the individual does not allow men to be the slaves of error and of passion, the worst of all masters; which, too, in public administration guides the citizens in wisdom and provides for them increased means of well-being; and which, further, protects the State from foreign interference [IMMORTALE DEI, 37].

License takes on many forms of expression. Pope Leo makes this comment:

We cannot look on an audacious disdain of all legitimate power as a perfection of civil life. Neither can we salute by the name of liberty the pursuit of a disgraceful and unhappy course that leads to the unchecked propagation of errors, the unhindered satisfaction of the worst passions, the impunity with which crimes can be committed, and the oppression of honest citizens of every class. These are false, erroneous, and perverse principles. They can assuredly not help to render human nature perfect, or to make it more prosperous, for "sin maketh nations miserable" (Prov. xiv, 34). On the contrary, it is absolutely inevitable that these principles, after corrupting the spirits and minds of men, will by their natural influence precipitate the people into all sorts of misfortunes, so as to upturn all legitimate order, and sooner or later, end in the final destruction of the State and public tranquility [INSCRUTABILI, 6].

Errors to Be Avoided. When applied to economic life, liberty must be appraised with caution against erroneous evaluations.

Economic life means social life—the life of human beings. Hence it cannot be conceived without liberty. This liberty can never be the seductive but deceptive formula of 100 years ago [the Pope was writing in 1948]—the purely negative liberty derived from the regulating will of the State. Nor is it the pseudo-liberty of our day—the submission of oneself to the dictate of mighty organizations. Genuine and true liberty can only be that of men who feel themselves bound to the objective goal of social economy and enjoy the right to demand that economies be ordered socially so as to guarantee and protect liberty, rather than restrict even in least degree the choice of means to that end. This is true, and for the same reason, both for independent workers and for wage earners. As regards the end of the social economy, every productive member is the subject and not the object of economic life (Exchange, 422-423).

Contrary to the erroneous opinion of those who do not examine the matter carefully, there is no incompatibility between essential authority and liberty—whether in the State, the Industry Council Plan, or any other human association. When the movement Le Sillon offered a threat to the proper balance between authority and liberty, Pope Pius X pointed out the function of authority with particular emphasis since some of the members of the movement seemed to have lost sight of its importance. He showed the resulting anarchy which would obtain from a spurious triple emancipation—political, economic, and intellectual —advocated by those so confused, and then he posed this query:

Has not every society of creatures, independent and unequal by nature, need of an authority to direct their activity towards the common welfare and to impose upon it its law?

And if in society there are to be found perverse individuals (there will always be such), should not authority be all the stronger in proportion as the egotism of the wicked is more menacing? Can one believe, then, with a shadow of reason that there is incompatibility between authority and liberty, unless one greatly deceives oneself in the conception of liberty? Can one teach that obedience is contrary to human dignity and that the ideal would be to replace it by "accepted authority"? Had not the Apostle St. Paul in view human society in all its possible conditions when he bade the faithful be subject to every authority? Does obedience to men as the legitimate representatives of God, that is to say, in a word obedience to God, degrade man and reduce him to a level beneath himself? Can the religious State, founded upon obedience, be contrary to the ideal of human nature? Were the saints, who were the most obedient of men, slaves and degenerates? Finally, can one imagine a social state in which Jesus Christ, if he returned to the earth, would not give an example of obedience, and, further, would not say:

Render to Caesar the things that are Caesar's and to God the things that are God's (Sillon, 700)?

Authority as a Necessity. "Nor is any man permitted to rule himself by his own fancy. . . ." [SAPIENTIAE CHRISTIANAE, 9]. Thus liberty requires authority as a deterrent from degeneration into license.

This doctrine [of the dignity and authority of the State] is equally removed from all extremes of error and all exaggerations of parties or systems which stem from error. It maintains a constant equilibrium of truth and justice, which it vindicates in theory and applies and promotes in practice, bringing into harmony the rights and duties of all parties. Thus authority is reconciled with liberty, the dignity of the individual with that of the State, the human personality of the subject with the divine delegation of the superior; and in this way a balance is struck between the due dependence and well-ordered love of a man for himself, his family and country, and his love of other families and other peoples, founded on the love of God, the Father of all, their first principle and last end [DIVINI REDEMPTORIS, 34].

Liberty does not mean that every man can do "what he pleases":

From this it is manifest that the eternal law of God is the sole standard and rule of human liberty not only in each individual man, but also in the community and civil society which men constitute when united. Therefore, the true liberty of human society does not consist in every man doing what he pleases, for this would simply end in turmoil and confusion, and bring on the overthrow of the State; but rather in this, that through the injunctions of the civil law all may more easily conform to the prescriptions of the eternal law. Likewise, the liberty of those who are in authority does not consist in the power to lay unreasonable and capricious commands upon their subjects, which would equally be criminal and would lead to the ruin of the commonwealth. . . . [LIBERTAS PRAE-STANTISSIMUM, 7].

In line with this thought Pope Leo gives this warning:

. . . the nature of human liberty, however it be considered, whether in individuals or in society, whether in those who command or in those who obey, supposes the necessity of obe-dience to some supreme and eternal law, which is no other than the authority of God, commanding good and forbidding evil. And, so far from this most just authority of God over men diminishing, or even destroying their liberty, it protects and perfects it; for the real perfection of all creatures is found in the prosecution and attainment of their respective ends. But the supreme end to which human liberty must aspire is God [LIBERTAS PRAESTANTISSIMUM, 8].

For freedom of action to be possible, order must be maintained:

Likewise, much was said of the state of liberty . . . liberty triumphing over despotism and over violence. But this cannot flourish except where justice and law command and effica-ciously secure the respect for individual and collective dignity.

Meanwhile, the world is still waiting and pleading that jus-tice and law create stable conditions for man and society (Name Day 1947, 451).

In a particular organization, such as the Industry Coun-cil Plan, the words of Pope Pius X are applicable.

A certain freedom of organization should be allowed them ["varied organizations"], for it is not possible, when many persons meet together, that all should be modelled on the same pattern or follow one single direction. Their organization should spring spontaneously from the works themselves; otherwise they will be like buildings of fine architecture, but without solid foundations, and therefore quite unstable.

It is also necessary to take into account the natural disposition of separate populations. Different usages and tendencies are found in different places. The important thing is to have a good foundation of solid principles, maintained with earnestness and constancy, and if this be the case, the method and form of the various works will be only accidental [IL FERMO PROPOSITO, p. 198].

It is liberty of this caliber, true liberty, which is essential to the establishment of the Industry Council Plan.

Chapter VI

Self-Government

ANOTHER ESSENTIAL ELEMENT in the Industry Council System is self-government—the fourth principle in our enumeration. In QUADRAGESIMO ANNO, Pope Pius XI sets forth the form of government for a socio-economic system:

The teaching of Leo XIII on the form of political government, namely, that men are free to choose whatever form they please, provided that proper regard is had for the requirements of justice and of the common good, is equally applicable in due proportion, it is hardly necessary to say, to the guilds of the various industries and professions [QUADRAGESIMO ANNO, 86].

That this form of government should be democratic may be implied from Pope Pius XII's 1944 Christmas message in which, speaking of democracy in general, he says: "If . . . then we consider the extent and nature of the sacrifices demanded of all the citizens, especially in our day when the activity of the State is so vast and decisive, the democratic form of government appears to many as a postulate of nature imposed by reason itself" (Christmas 1944, 67-68).

Its Basis: Right of Association. Self-government flows from the right of association as means to an end. This right of association has been insisted on repeatedly by the Popes. Pope Pius XI in listing rights existing in consequence of man's relation to God and His Divine plan names the right of association (infra p. 117, DIVINI REDEMPTORIS, 27). Again in QUADRAGESIMO ANNO he states the following:

People are quite free not only to found such associations, which are a matter of private order and private right, but also in respect to them "freely to adopt the organization and the rules which they judge most appropriate to achieve their purpose." The same freedom must be asserted for founding associations that go beyond the boundaries of individual callings [QUADRAGESIMO ANNO, 87].

Pope Pius XII elaborates on this truth:

Because sociability is one of man's natural requirements and since it is legitimate to promote by common effort decent livelihood, it is not possible without injustice to deny or to limit either to the producers or to the laboring and farming classes the free faculty of uniting in associations by means of which they may defend their proper rights and secure the betterment of the goods of soul and of body, as well as the honest comforts of life [SERTUM LAETITIAE, 39].

On this point Pope Pius XI issues another indictment of Liberalism when he scores the heads of the States who

. . . imbued with Liberalism, were showing little favor to workers' associations of this type; nay, rather they openly opposed them, and while going out of their way to recognize similar organizations of other classes and show favor to them, they were with criminal injustice denying the natural right to form associations to those who needed it most to defend themselves from ill treatment at the hands of the powerful [QUADRAGESIMO ANNO, 30].

When associations are under the control of evil leaders who employ principles contrary to Christianity and public well-being in an attempt to gain monopoly of leadership over labor, Pope Leo XIII tells us that Christian workmen then have a duty to organize in associations.

Under these circumstances, workers who are Christians must choose one of two things: either to join associations in which it is greatly to be feared that there is danger to religion, or to form their own associations and unite their forces in such a way that they may be able manfully to free themselves from such unjust and intolerable oppression. Can they who refuse to place man's highest good in imminent jeopardy hesitate to affirm that the second course is by all means to be followed [RERUM NOVARUM, 74]?

Limitations on the Right. Pope Leo XIII points out limitations to the right of association:

Occasionally there are times when it is proper for the laws to oppose associations of this kind, that is, if they professedly seek after any objective which is clearly at variance with good morals, with justice or with the welfare of the State. Indeed, in these cases the public power shall justly prevent such associations from forming and shall also justly dissolve those already formed. Nevertheless, it must use the greatest precaution lest it appear to infringe on the rights of its citizens, and lest, under the pretext of public benefit, it enact any measure that sound reason would not support. For laws are to be obeyed only insofar as they conform with right reason and thus with the eternal law of God [RERUM NOVARUM, 72].

Limitations on Unions. Pope Pius XII indicates principles which must be obeyed by unions in the exercise of their self-government.

But let the unions in question draw their vital force from principles of wholesome liberty; let them take their form from the lofty rules of justice and of honesty and, conforming themselves to those norms, let them act in such a manner that in their care for the interests of their class they violate no one's rights; let them continue to strive for harmony and respect the common weal of civil society [SERTUM LAETITIAE, 40].

Kind of Self-Government. As to the kind of self-government, both Pope Leo XIII and Pope Pius XI advise flexibility.

Unquestionably, wise direction and organization are essential to these associations in order that in their activities there be unity of purpose and concord of wills. Furthermore, if citizens have free right to associate, as in fact they do, they also must have the right freely to adopt the organization and the rules which they judge most appropriate to achieve their purpose. We do not feel that the precise character in all details which the aforementioned direction and organization of associations ought to have can be determined by fast and fixed rules, since this is a matter to be decided rather in the light of the temperament of each people, of experiment and practice, of the nature and character of the work, of the extent of trade and commerce, and of other circumstances of a material and temporal kind, all of which must be carefully considered. In summary, let this be laid down as a general and constant law: Workers' associations ought to be so constituted and so governed as to furnish the most suitable and most convenient means to attain the object proposed, which consists in this, that the individual members of the association secure, so far as possible, an increase in the goods of body, of soul, and of prosperity [RERUM NOVARUM, 76].

Method of Self-Government. The method to be employed is indicated in QUADRAGESIMO ANNO.

Concerning matters, however, in which particular points, involving advantage or detriment to employers or workers, may require special care and protection, the two parties, when these cases arise, can deliberate separately or as the situation requires reach a decision separately [QUADRAGESIMO ANNO, 85].

Details to be Handled. Pope Leo XIII indicates details that are fit subjects to be handled by the members of the association in their exercise of self-government:

Offices in the associations are to be distributed properly in accordance with the common interest, and in such a way, moreover, that wide difference in these offices may not create discord. It is of special importance that obligations be apportioned wisely and be clearly defined, to the end that no one is done an injustice. Let the funds be disbursed equitably in such way that the amount of benefit to be paid out to members is fixed beforehand in accordance with individual needs, and let the rights and duties of employers be properly adjusted to the rights and duties of workers. If any one in these two groups feels that he has been injured in any way, nothing is more to be desired than that prudent and upright men of the same body be available, and that the association regulations themselves prescribe that the dispute be settled according to the decision of these men.
It must also be specially provided that the worker at no time be without sufficient work, and that the monies paid into the

treasury of the association furnish the means of assisting individual members in need, not only during sudden and unforeseen changes in industry, but also whenever anyone is stricken by sickness, by old age, or by misfortune [RERUM NOVARUM, 78-79].

A right proportion among wages and salaries also contributes directly to the same result; and with this is closely connected a right proportion in the prices at which the goods are sold that are produced by the various occupations, such as agriculture, manufacturing, and others. If all these relations are properly maintained, the various occupations will combine and coalesce into, as it were, a single body and like members of the body mutually aid and complete one another. For then only will the social economy be rightly established and attain its purposes when all and each are supplied with all the goods that the wealth and resources of nature, technical achievement, and the social organization of economic life can furnish. And these goods ought indeed to be enough both to meet the demands of necessity and decent comfort and to advance people to that happier and fuller condition of life which, when it is wisely cared for, is not only no hindrance to virtue but helps it greatly [QUADRAGESIMO ANNO, 75].

Unions' Share in Management. After showing that the wage contract is not inherently unjust, Pope Pius XI, nevertheless, urges the advisability of a contract of partnership which would bring the present organization closer to the Industry Council system.

We consider it more advisable, however, in the present condition of human society that, so far as is possible, the work-contract be somewhat modified by a partnership-contract, as is already being done in various ways and with no small advantage to workers and owners. Workers and other employees thus become sharers in ownership or management or participate in some fashion in the profits received [QUADRAGESIMO ANNO, 65].

In 1951, Pope Pius XII took substantially the same position.

She [the Church] regards with approval and favors everything which, within the limits permitted by circumstances, aims at introducing the elements of a partnership contract (*contrato de sociedad*) into the wage contract (*contrato de trabajo*), and betters the general condition of the worker. The Church likewise counsels all to use whatever contributes toward making relations between employer and workers more human, more Christian and more conducive to mutual confidence. The class struggle can never be a social end. The discussions between employers and workers must have as their main aim peace and collaboration (Spanish Employers and Workers, 707).

And in 1952 Pope Pius XII speaks more urgently.

. . . if both employers and workers have a common interest in the healthy prosperity of the national economy, why should it not be legitimate to give to the workers a just share of responsibility in the organization and development of that economy (Semaines 1952, 12)?

In the same discourse Our Holy Father gives an added reason for workers sharing responsibility.

This remark [quoted above], which We [also] made in Our address of May 7, 1949, is all the more opportune now when under the difficulties, insecurities, and joint liabilities which mark the present time, a country must sometimes make economic decisions which will affect the whole future of the national community and often even the future of the whole family of nations (Semaines 1952, 12).

Pope Leo XIII had also pointed out the necessity of protection against injustice and infers the part unions should play:

Let it be granted then that worker and employer may enter freely into agreements and, in particular, concerning the amount of the wage; yet there is always underlying such agreements an element of natural justice, and one greater and more ancient than the free consent of contracting parties, namely, that the wage shall not be less than enough to support a worker who is thrifty and upright. If, compelled by necessity or moved by fear of a worse evil, a worker accepts a harder condition, which although against his will he must accept because the employer or contractor imposes it, he certainly submits to force, against which justice cries out in protest [RERUM NOVARUM, 63].

Again, in QUADRAGESIMO ANNO, Pope Pius XI has this to say:

Let, then, both workers and employers strive with united strength and counsel to overcome the difficulties and obstacles and let a wise provision on the part of public authority aid them in so salutary a work. If, however, matters come to an extreme crisis, it must be finally considered whether the business can continue or the workers are to be cared for in some other way. In such a situation, certainly most serious, a feeling of close relationship and a Christian concord of minds ought to prevail and function effectively among employers and workers [QUADRAGESIMO ANNO, 73].

The need for such share in management is seen from the inadequacy of a social policy which had, as one of its main tenets, the strengthening of labor's position by social legislation. In 1950, Pope Pius XII pointed this out in these words:

For several decades now, in the majority of these countries and often under the decisive influence of the Catholic social movement, social policy has been taking the form of a progressive evolution in labor legislation, with a corresponding subjection of the private owner of the means of production to juridical obligations in favor of the workingman. The desire to see social policy further developed along these lines encounters a limit, and that limit is reached where the danger arises that the working class may follow in its turn the mistaken course of capital. That course involved the withdrawing of personal responsibility, chiefly in big business, from the private owner (individual or partnership) and handing it over to the responsibility of anonymous corporate groups.

Such a development would suit a Socialist mentality to perfection. It could not but prove disturbing to anyone who is aware of the fundamental importance of the right to private property in stimulating initiative and fixing responsibility in economic matters (Production, 508).

Earlier, in his allocution to Belgian workers, the Pope cited this as a threat to the worker's movement.

[There is a] danger which at present, in some degree, everywhere threatens the worker's movement. We mean the temptation to abuse. We speak of abuse and certainly not of the legitimate use—the strength of the organization. This temptation is just as formidable and dangerous as that of abusing the strength of private capital. To expect from such an abuse the attainment of stable conditions for the State and for society would be both for one side and the other a vain illusion, not to say blindness and folly—an illusion and folly doubly fatal for the well-being and the freedom of the worker, who would himself be hurled into slavery (Belgian Workers, 60-61).

Co-operation and unity should supplant mutual distrust and an unfair kind of competition.

This duty, this ideal, is the full, the lofty, the Christian management of your establishment, penetrated with human sentiments in the widest and highest sense of the word. Like the drop of oil in the gears, this humane sense must penetrate all the members and all the branches of industry: the executives, the assistants, the clerical employes, and the workers of all ranks from the most highly skilled artisan to the lowest worker.

If business firms, effectively penetrated with the truly human spirit, multiply and unite with you one after another, they will become so many large families. If not content with their own separate existence, as in a closed vase, they will unite among themselves all together, they will tend to form a strong and happy society (Italian Employers, 570).

Granted that workers should share in management, how far should this sharing go? Pope Pius XII provides the answers, first, in respect to management; second, in respect to production. In his 1949 address to Catholic Employers, he made this statement:

All that We have just said applies to the juridical nature of the enterprise as such. But the business may involve a whole category of other personnel relationships which must be taken into account—even those of shared responsibility. The owner of the means of production, whoever he be—individual owner, workers' association or corporation—must always—within the limits of public economic law—retain control of his economic decisions. It goes without saying that his income is higher than that of his collaborators. But it follows that the material prosperity of the entire population, which is the objective of social economy, lays upon him, more than upon the others, the obligation of contributing by savings to the increase of the nation's fund of capital. As we must not forget, on the other hand, that it is supremely advantageous to a healthy social economy when this accumulation of capital derives from the greatest possible number of sources, it is very desirable, in consequence, that the workmen also should be enabled, by the fruit of their savings, to share in the creation of the capital resources of their country (Employers, 447).

Joint-Management, Joint-Ownership. In his address of June 3, 1950, the Pope discussed the question of economic joint-management, referred to currently as co-determination, in industry. Pertinent passages, which have been interpreted differently by different authorities, follow.

A similar danger is likewise present when it is claimed that the wage-earners in a given industry have the right to economic joint-management, notably when the exercise of this right rests in reality, directly or indirectly, with organizations managed from outside the establishment.

As a matter of fact, neither the nature of the labor contract nor the nature of the business enterprise in themselves admit necessarily of a right of this sort. It is unquestionable that the wage-earner and the employer are equally the subjects, not the objects, of a nation's economy. There is no question of denying this parity. It is already an established principle of social policy; it would be asserted still more effectively were that policy to be organized on the occupational level. But there is nothing in the private-law relationship, as governed by the simple wage-contract, to contradict this fundamental parity.

The wisdom of Our Predecessor Pius XI has made that quite clear in the Encyclical QUADRAGESIMO ANNO, where he denies, in consequence, that there is any need in the nature of things to pattern the wage-contract on the contract of partnership. This is not to disavow the usefulness of what has thus far been achieved in this direction, "in various ways, to the no small gain of both wage-earners and employers" (*Acta Apostolicae Sedis,* vol. 23, p. 199). But in the light of principles and facts the right of economic joint-management lies beyond the field of these possible achievements.

The disadvantage of these problems lies in the fact that they make one lose sight of the problem of major importance and major urgency which broods like a nightmare especially over the old industrial countries, that is, the imminent and permanent menace of unemployment, the problem of the reintegration and maintenance of normal productive enterprise, of that productivity which is intimately linked, by its origin as well as in its purpose, to the dignity and well-being of the family viewed as a moral, juridical, and economic unit (Production, 508-509).

Two Pitfalls. After noting the progress made in spreading a knowledge of social thought through the efforts of the Church and leading thinkers, Pope Pius XII in his address to the Austrian Catholic Convention (Katholikentag) in 1952 outlines the questions and tasks of the next phase of the social dispute into which he believes we are entering. The two points he discusses relate to the questions of joint-ownership and joint-management and the danger of distorting the worker's rights by proceeding on a false basis of collectivist philosophy. His Holiness points out, first, that an organic union of labor and management *against* the rest of society is contrary to the nature of man and violates the principle of organic unity of all society:

The overcoming of the class struggle through an organic co-ordination of employer and employee for class struggle can never be a goal of Catholic social ethics. The Church is always aware of its duties toward all classes and layers of the people (Katholikentag, 14).

Secondly, in the question of labor sharing in the owner-ship of operating capital and in participating in decisions regarding the operation of an industry, the Pope warns against the violation of the human dignity of the individual and the family together with the corollary right of private property:

In the second place, the protection of the individual and of the family against the vortex which threatens to draw them into an all-embracing socialization, at the end of which looms the very real nightmare of "Leviathan." The Church will con-duct this fight to the utmost, because the highest things are at stake—human dignity and the salvation of the soul.

It is for this reason that Catholic social teaching, besides other things, so emphatically champions the right of the indi-vidual to own property. Herein also lie the deeper motives why the Pontiffs of the social encyclicals, and also We Ourselves, have declined to deduce directly or indirectly, from the labor contract the right of the employee to partake in the ownership of the operating capital, and its corollary, the right of the worker to participate in decisions concerning operations of the plant.

This had to be denied because behind this question there stands that greater problem. The right of the individual and of the family to own property stems immediately from the human person, it is a right of personal dignity; a right, to be sure, accompanied by social obligations; it is, however, a right, not merely a social function (Katholikentag, 14).

Fidelity to Correct Social Ethics. Our Holy Father then exhorts us to maintain a careful fidelity to the true Catholic social teaching in order to avoid the pitfalls of error following upon a slight deviation from true social ethics:

We feel compelled to exhort you and all other Catholics anew, to hew to the clearly defined line of Catholic social teaching from the very beginning of the new dispute, without deviating to the right or to the left. A deviation from that line, even if only by a few degrees, may at first seem inconsequential. However, in the long run it would lead dangerously astray from the right path and bring fateful consequences. Calm thinking, self-control, steadfastness in the face of temptations from either extreme must, then, be a watchword of the hour (Katholikentag, 14).

Progress Made. QUADRAGESIMO ANNO notes some progress and a trend in the direction of greater self-government and "mutual co-operation" in line with correct social ethics.

For if the class struggle abstains from enmities and mutual hatred, it gradually changes into an honest discussion of differences founded on a desire for justice, and if that is not that blessed social peace which we all seek, it can and ought to be the point of departure from which to move forward to the mutual co-operation of the Industries and Professions [QUAD-RAGESIMO ANNO, 114].

Chapter VII

Graded Structure

Graded Priority. The principle of graded structure, the proper order of the parts of the social organism, is necessary for tranquillity and order. This principle demands a respect for rights together with a recognition of a graded priority.*

For He who created and governs all things has, in His wise providence, appointed that the things which are lowest should attain their ends by those which are intermediate, and these again by the highest. Thus, as even in the kingdom of heaven He hath willed that the choirs of angels be distinct and some

* Trehey explains: "Therefore, because there are different degrees of authority it can readily be seen that, while each group must possess autonomy in order to attain fully its particular objective, at the same time there must be subordination of authority among these groups in proportion to their contribution to the general objective. Order, being an apt arrangement of a multiplicity of parts, demands that certain parts of the social organism have rights superior to those of other parts. Otherwise, the constant conflict of group with group, on the question of rights would bring about a condition in society that would be the very negation of peace and order. Hence, 'we have a subordination, and super-ordination of the multifarious authorities in society which we designate as the Principle of Graded Structure'" (Harold Francis Trehey, *Foundations of a Modern Guild System*, Washington: Catholic University of America Press, 1940, p. 56).

subject to others, and in the Church likewise has instituted various orders and a diversity of offices, so that all are not apostles or doctors or pastors (I Cor. xii), so also has He appointed that there should be various orders in civil society, differing in dignity, rights, and power, whereby the State, like the Church, should be one body, consisting of many members, some nobler than others, but all necessary to each other and solicitous for the common good [QUOD APOSTOLICI MUNERIS, 6].

If social life implies intrinsic unity, it does not, at the same time, exclude differences which are founded in fact and nature. When we hold fast to God, the Supreme Controller of all that relates to man, then the similarities no less than the differences of men find their allotted place in the fixed order of being, of values, and hence also of morality (Christmas 1942, 5-6).

Distinction in Classes. In line with this principle also the Popes recognized distinction in classes—but not unjust discrimination. "It is not true that all have equal rights in civil society. It is not true that there exists no lawful social hierarchy" [DIVINI REDEMPTORIS, 33].

Therefore, let it be laid down in the first place that a condition of human existence must be borne with, namely, that in civil society the lowest cannot be made equal with the highest. Socialists, of course, agitate the contrary, but all struggling against nature is vain. There are truly very great and very many natural differences among men. Neither the talents, nor the skill, nor the health, nor the capacities of all are the same, and unequal fortune follows of itself upon necessary inequality in respect to these endowments. And clearly this condition of things is adapted to benefit both individuals and the community; for to carry on its affairs community life requires varied aptitudes and diverse services. . . . [RERUM NOVARUM, 26].

Question of Equality. In the light of these necessary inequalities, how is it possible to attain the union and brotherhood necessary for the reorganization of society? In what sense are all men equal?

In a people worthy of the name all inequalities based not on whim but on the nature of things, inequalities of culture, possessions, social standing—without of course prejudice to justice and mutual charity—do not constitute any obstacle to the existence and the prevalence of a true spirit of union and brotherhood.

On the contrary, so far from impairing civil equality in any way, they give it its true meaning, namely, that, before the State, everyone has the right to live honorably his own personal life in the place and under the conditions in which the designs and dispositions of Providence have placed him (Christmas 1944, 68-69).

. . . in accordance with the teachings of the Gospel, the equality of man consists in this: that all, having inherited the same nature, are called to the same most high dignity of the sons of God; and that, as one and the same end is set before all, each one is to be judged by the same law and will receive punishment or reward according to his deserts. The inequality of rights and of power proceeds from the very Author of nature, "from whom all paternity in heaven and earth is named" (Eph. iii, 15). But the minds of princes and their subjects are, according to Catholic doctrine and precepts, bound up one with the other in such a manner, by mutual duties and rights, that the license of power is restrained and the rational ground of obedience made easy, firm, and noble [QUOD APOSTOLICI MUNERIS, 5].

Inclusion of All. Christian Democracy involves "the natural co-ordination of the working classes with the other ranks of society."

It is large enough to embrace all ranks as belonging to one and the same family, the offspring of the same all-beneficent Father, redeemed by one Saviour, and called to the same eternal inheritance. This is, indeed, the Apostle's doctrine and monition: *One body and one Spirit, as you are called in one hope of your calling; one Lord, one faith, one baptism; one God and Father of all, who is above all, and through all, and in us all* (Eph. iv. 4-6). Wherefore, because of the natural co-ordination of the working classes with the other ranks of society, which is made more intimate by the law of Christian brotherhood, it surely follows that whatever diligence is bestowed upon assisting the working classes must extend to these other classes—the more because it is clearly proper and even necessary, if the work is to be successful, as we shall show below, that they should be invited to take part in it [GRAVES DE COMMUNI, 172-173].

Graded Structure Necessary. Pope Pius XII called attention to the necessity for a graded structure in society:

By contrast, those who would make of society and State a mere conglomeration of laboring-men, disregard the fundamental nature of labor and civil society. Labor is emptied of its real meaning and denied its inward unifying power (Semaines, 1947, 682).

But it is only the moral law which, just as it commands us to seek our supreme and last end in the whole scheme of our activity, so likewise commands us to seek directly in each kind of activity those purposes which we know that nature, or rather God the Author of nature, established for that kind of action, and in orderly relationship to subordinate such immediate purposes to our supreme and last end. If we faithfully observe this law, then it will follow that the particular purposes, both individual and social, that are sought in the economic field will fall in their proper place in the universal order of purposes, and We, in ascending through them, as it were by steps, shall attain the final end of all things, that is God, to Himself and to us, the supreme and inexhaustible Good [QUADRAGESIMO ANNO, 43].

On International Level. And, finally, graded structure should be extended to an international level.

Furthermore, since the various nations largely depend on one another in economic matters and need one another's help, they should strive with a united purpose and effort to promote by wisely conceived pacts and institutions a prosperous and happy international co-operation in economic life [QUADRAGESIMO ANNO, 89].

National economy, being the economy of a people within the unity of the State, is itself a natural unity. It requires the most harmonious development possible of all means of production within the territory covered by the nation. Accordingly, international economic relations have a function which, although positive and necessary, is only subsidiary. The upsetting of this relationship between national and international economy was one of the great errors of the past. Today the circumstances under which a large number of people are forced to live could easily favor the return of unsettled conditions. At this juncture, it would perhaps be opportune to examine whether or not a regional union of different national economies would render possible a more efficacious development of the forces of production (Exchange, 423).

As an application of this principle then, the Industry Council Plan must be conceived as not only organized on local, regional, and national levels, but also on the international level. (See charts, pp. 6, 7).

Chapter VIII

Public-Legal Status

Associations Compared to Municipalities. That the Popes have in mind a public-legal status for industry councils is borne out by the fact that repeatedly they speak of the juridical nature of free and private associations which should "set before themselves the task of preparing the way . . . for those larger and more important guilds, Industries, and Professions" [QUADRAGESIMO ANNO, 87]. The Popes liken these free associations to municipalities which exercise power to enforce law.

Moreover, just as inhabitants of a town are wont to found associations with the widest diversity of purposes, which each is quite free to join or not, so those engaged in the same industry or profession will combine with one another into associations equally free for purposes connected in some manner with the pursuit of the calling itself [QUADRAGESIMO ANNO, 87].

It [spirit of cold egoism] must be supplanted by sincere juridical and economic solidarity, fraternal collaboration in accordance with the precepts of Divine law amongst peoples assured of their autonomy and independence (Christmas 1940, 6).

Drafting of Public Law Needed. In 1949, Pope Pius XII reminded the Belgian workers that "the strength of an organization . . . is not of itself an element of order," a proposition evident from the observation of totalitarianism. Rather, correct order comes from building on the foundations laid down by the Creator and "This is why We never tire of recommending the immediate drafting of a public law covering economic life and all society, according to the organization of industries and professions" (Belgian Workers, 61). Until such a law is drafted to inaugurate some order, such as the Industry Council system, public-legal status as such does not exist, and the enterprise "falls within the competence of the private-law discipline of economic life."

Error to Be Avoided. Pope Pius XII pointed out an error to be avoided:

It would be . . . untrue to assert that every particular business is of its nature a society, with its personnel relationships determined by the norms of distributive justice to the point where all without distinction—owners or not of the means of production—would be entitled to their share in the property, or at the very least in the profits, of the enterprise. Such a conception stems from the assumption that every business belongs naturally within the sphere of public law. The assumption is inexact. Whether the business is organized in the form of a corporation or an association of all the workmen as part-owners, or whether it is the private property of an individual who signs a wage-contract with all his employees, in the one case as in the other it falls within the competence of the private-law discipline of economic life (Employers, 447).

Fascist Corporations Criticized. Pope Leo warns us that "man is older than the State. Wherefore he had to possess by nature his own right to protect his life and body before any polity had been formed" [RERUM NOVARUM, 13]. The making of the industry council a political tool of the State rather than an instrument for the general welfare and social order is a major criticism levelled by Pope Pius XI against the Fascist corporations.

Yet lest We neglect anything in a matter of such great importance and that all points treated may be properly connected with the more general principles which We mentioned above and with those which We intend shortly to add, We are compelled to say that to Our certain knowledge there are not wanting some who fear that the State, instead of confining itself as it ought to the furnishing of necessary and adequate assistance, is substituting itself for free activity; that the new syndical and corporative order savors too much of an involved and political system of administration; and that (in spite of those more general advantages mentioned above, which are of course fully admitted) it rather serves particular political ends than leads to the reconstruction and promotion of a better social order [QUADRAGESIMO ANNO, 95].

Pope Pius XII again agrees with Pope Pius XI in urging that the new order be inaugurated by law.

Our Predecessor of imperishable memory, Pius XI, had suggested the practical and timely prescription for this community of interest in the nation's economic enterprise when he recommended in his Encyclical QUADRAGESIMO ANNO "occupational organization" for the various branches of production. Nothing, indeed, appeared to him more suited to bring economic liberalism under control than the enactment, for the social economy, of a public-law statute based precisely on the common responsibility which is shared by all those who take part in production. This feature of the Encyclical stirred up a host of objections. Some saw in it a concession to modern political trends, while for others it meant a return to the Middle Ages. It would have been incomparably more sensible to lay aside the flimsy prejudices of the past and to get down to work sincerely and courageously to make the proposal, with its many practical applications, a living reality (Employers, 446).

Chapter IX

General Welfare

ANOTHER KEY PRINCIPLE in the reorganization of society through the establishment of the Industry Council Plan is that of the general welfare or the common good. Pope Pius XII says "That good can neither be defined according to arbitrary ideas nor can it accept for its standard primarily the material prosperity of society, but rather it should be defined according to the harmonious development and the natural perfection of man" [SUMMI PONTIFICATUS, 54]. This perfection involves all those things which develop man physically, intellectually, and morally. In DIVINI REDEMPTORIS Pope Pius XI reminds us that "it must likewise be the special care of the State to create those material conditions of life without which an orderly society cannot exist" [DIVINI REDEMPTORIS, 75].

. . . the whole political and economic activity of the State is directed to the permanent realization of the common good. It is to create those external conditions which are needed for the mass of the citizens, to bring their natural virtues to maturity, to fulfill their office and develop fully their material, intellectual, and religious life. . . . (Christmas 1942, 6).

74

"It is for this perfection that society is designed by the Creator as a means" [SUMMI PONTIFICATUS, 54]. "Men live in a civic society not only for their own good, but also for the good of all. . . ." [GRAVES DE COMMUNI, 177].

When describing the unity of the Church in the Mystical Body, Pope Pius XII shows by analogy how the general welfare is fostered. This same analogy may be applied to the social organization called for in the Industry Council Plan.

But a body calls also for a multiplicity of members, which are linked together in such a way as to help one another. And as in the body when one member suffers, all the other members share its pain, and the healthy members come to the assistance of the ailing, so in the Church the individual members do not live for themselves alone, but also help their fellows, and all work in mutual collaboration for the common comfort and for the more perfect building up of the whole Body [MYSTICI CORPORIS CHRISTI, 15].

It [the Church] alone, in fact, with Divine mission and of Divine command, teaches that all human actions, public or private, individual or collective, must conform to the eternal law of God. And it is clear that such actions as affect the good of great numbers are of the far greatest importance [UBI ARCANO DEI, 307].

Rooted in Man's Nature. This general welfare has its roots in man's nature, "with his harmonious co-ordination of personal rights and social obligations."

. . . the basic fact [is] that man as a person possesses God-given rights, which must be preserved from all attacks aimed at denying, suppressing, or disregarding them. To pay no heed to this truth is to overlook the fact that the true public good is finally determined and recognized by the nature of man, with his harmonious co-ordination of personal rights and social obligations, as well as by the purpose of the community which in turn is conditioned by the same human nature. The community is willed by the Creator as the means to the full development of the individual and social attainments, which the individual in give and take has to employ to his own good and that of others. Also those higher and more comprehensive values, that cannot be realized by the individual but only by the community, in the final analysis are intended by the Creator for the sake of the individual, for his natural and supernatural development and perfection. A deviation from this order loosens the supports on which the community is placed, and thereby imperils the tranquillity, security, and even the existence of the community itself [MIT BRENNENDER SORGE, 35].

Universal Responsibility. The general welfare derives its fundamental importance from the fact that "it is of the very essence of social justice to demand from each individual all that is necessary for the common good" [DIVINI REDEMPTORIS, 51]. ". . . one's work ought to contribute to the common good; it should testify to the sense of responsibility of each for the well-being of all" (Bank of Italy, 332).

Those in Government. This universal responsibility which requires that each of us further the general welfare is applied by the Sovereign Pontiffs to those in government.

Although all citizens, without exception, are obliged to contribute something to the sum-total common goods, some share of which naturally goes back to each individual, yet all can by no means contribute the same amount and in equal degree. Whatever the vicissitudes that occur in the forms of government, there will always be those differences in the condition of citizens without which society could neither exist nor be conceived. It is altogether necessary that there be some who dedicate themselves to the service of the State, who make laws, who dispense justice, and finally, by whose counsel and authority civil and military affairs are administered. These men, as is clear, play the chief role in the State, and among every people are to be regarded as occupying first place, because they work for the common good most directly and preeminently. On the other hand, those engaged in some calling benefit the State, but not in the same way as the men just mentioned, nor by performing the same duties; yet they, too, in a high degree, although less directly, serve the public weal. Assuredly, since social good must be of such a character that men through its acquisition are made better, it must necessarily be founded chiefly on virtue [RERUM NOVARUM, 50].

Unless it be otherwise determined, by reason of some exceptional condition of things, it is expedient to take part in the administration of public affairs. And the Church approves of every one devoting his services to the common good, and doing all that he can for the defence, preservation, and prosperity of his country [LIBERTAS PRAESTANTISSIMUM, 33].

Businessmen and the Wealthy. Those in business, and the wealthy in general, are also admonished "to place the common welfare above their private advantage and profits":

Further, you will not obtain the goal you wish, which is the general prosperity, without putting into full effect the individual exercise of commerce for the service of society's material well-being. The merchant, one will say, should be skilled without doubt; he must be a man of affairs, prudent more than sentimental, again, without doubt. But he must add to these strictly professional qualities a high concept of the ideal of his profession. As a businessman, he must also consider himself a servant of the community.

To have no other ambition except always to make more money and to enrich himself, is to betray his vocation, since one can well call by this name [vocation] the mission that God has assigned to him, the particularly difficult calling of a merchant (Businessmen, 511).

At the same time it is the duty of all to realize that the world crisis is so serious today and so menacing for the future that it is imperative for all, especially the rich, to place the common welfare above their private advantage and profits [OPTATISSIMA PAX, p. 66].

It [social doctrine of the Church] demands of them especially a radical reaction against the temptation to seek each one's own advantage at the expense of the other partners—whatever be the nature and form of their participation—and to the detriment of the common welfare. It calls finally for unselfishness of a sort which can only be instilled by an authentic Christian virtue, sustained and aided by the grace of God (Employers, 448).

Institutions. The responsibility to further the general welfare rests on *all*, the individual as noted above, public institutions, associations, and unions. Common interests "should hold first place."

The public institutions themselves, of peoples, moreover, ought to make all human society conform to the needs of the common good; that is, to the norm of social justice. If this is done, that most important division of social life, namely, economic activity, cannot fail likewise to return to right and sound order [QUADRAGESIMO ANNO, 110].

It is easily deduced from what has been said that the interests common to the whole Industry or Profession should hold first place in these guilds. The most important among these interests is to promote the co-operation in the highest degree of each Industry and Profession for the sake of the common good of the country [QUADRAGESIMO ANNO, 85].

Farmers. Farmers' organizations, an integral part of an economic order, likewise must foster the general welfare.

At all events, continue to esteem your [agricultural] work according to its fundamental value, namely, as your contribution and that of your families to the public weal. On this is based your right to a return sufficient to enable you to live in a manner befitting your dignity as men and adequate also to provide for your cultural needs. It is moreover important that you should recognize the necessity for union with all the other professional or vocational groups that are supplying the various needs of the people, and thus signify your adherence to the principle of social peace (Farmer, 446).

Means to Be Employed. Means to be employed include God-given talents and charity.

. . . whoever has received from the bounty of God a greater share of goods, whether corporeal and external, or of the soul, has received them for this purpose, namely, that he employ them for his own perfection and, likewise, as a servant of Divine Providence, for the benefit of others. "Therefore, he that hath talent, let him constantly see to it that he be not silent; he that hath an abundance of goods, let him be on the watch that he grow not slothful in the generosity of mercy;

he that hath a trade whereby he supports himself, let him be especially eager to share with his neighbor the use and benefit thereof" (St. Gregory the Great, *In Evang. Hom. IX*, 7) [RERUM NOVARUM, 36].

Certainly, the well-being which is so longed for is chiefly to be expected from an abundant outpouring of charity; of Christian charity, We mean, which is in epitome the law of the Gospel, and which, always ready to sacrifice itself for the benefit of others, is man's surest antidote against the insolence of the world and immoderate love of self; the divine office and features of this virtue being described by the Apostle Paul in these words: "Charity is patient, is kind . . . is not self-seeking . . . bears with all things . . . endures all things" (I Cor. 13:4-7) [RERUM NOVARUM, 83].

The proper use of property is included in means:

But not every distribution among human beings of property and wealth is of a character to attain either completely or to a satisfactory degree of perfection the end which God intends. Therefore, the riches that economic-social developments constantly increase ought to be so distributed among individual persons and classes that the common advantage of all, which Leo XIII had praised, will be safeguarded; in other words, that the common good of all society will be kept inviolate. By this law of social justice, one class is forbidden to exclude the other from sharing in the benefits [QUADRAGESIMO ANNO, 57].

Pope Pius XII criticizes capitalism on this very point:

Accordingly where, for instance, "Capitalism" is based on such false concepts and arrogates to itself an unlimited right over property, without any subordination to the common good, the Church has condemned it as contrary to the natural law (Reconstruction, 580).

Thus, the principle of the general welfare must permeate the lives of the individuals and the associations. For additional statements relating to general welfare or the common good, see Chapter XII, "Man and Society; Social Justice; Moral Reform," infra, pp. 116 ff.

Chapter X

Limited State Intervention

Meaning. The principle of limited State intervention means that the State may step in to do the things which individuals or groups fail to do, when private initiative breaks down. This does not mean, however, that the duty and power of the State to procure the general welfare in economics comes to it only by default. The very legislation necessary to make industry councils self-governing is an exclusive function of the State and does not come to it by default.

When the State intervenes, it must respect individual activity:

To safeguard the inviolable sphere of the rights of the human person and to facilitate the fulfilment of his duties should be the essential office of every public authority. Does not this flow from that genuine concept of the common good which the State is called upon to promote?

Hence it follows that the care of such a common good does not imply a power so extensive over the members of the community that in virtue of it the public authority can interfere with the evolution of the individual activity which We have just described, decide on the beginning or the ending of human life, determine at will the manner of his physical, spiritual, religious, and moral movements in opposition to the personal duties or rights of men and to this end abolish or deprive of efficacy his natural rights to material goods.

To deduce such extension of power from the care of the common good would be equivalent to overthrowing the very meaning of the words "common good" and falling into the error that the proper scope of man on earth is society, that society is an end itself, that man has no other life which awaits him beyond that which ends here below (Pentecost, 9).

The finely balanced mean between possible extremes of too little or too much State intervention is also insisted upon by Pope Pius XII.

No one of good-will and vision will think of refusing the State, in the exceptional conditions of the world of today, correspondingly wider and exceptional rights to meet the popular needs. But even in such emergencies, the moral law, established by God, demands that the lawfulness of each such measure and its real necessity be scrutinized with the greatest rigor according to the standards of the common good [SUMMI PONTIFICATUS, 59].

Always remembering that ". . . the universal validity of 'reigning' lies in 'serving'" (Christmas 1942, 19).

Pope Pius XI summed up the powers of the State under four heads: directing, watching, urging, restraining. After laying down the principle of subsidiarity, he said: "Thereby the State will more freely, powerfully, and effectively do all those things which belong to it alone because it alone can do them: directing, watching, urging, restraining, as occasion requires and necessity demands" [QUADRAGESIMO ANNO, 80].

In the following pages, an attempt has been made to

group papal statements concerning State intervention under those four headings. There is some overlapping and there are some difficulties of interpretation. The reader should be cautioned that texts will not be repeated, however, but will be given only once, under the heading that seems most appropriate.

DIRECTING

Responsibility to Direct General Welfare. The State's responsibility for directing the general welfare is reiterated time and time again as we note in RERUM NOVARUM:

Therefore those governing the State ought primarily to devote themselves to the service of individual groups and of the whole commonwealth, and through the entire scheme of laws and institutions to cause both public and individual well-being to develop spontaneously out of the very structure and administration of the State. For this is the duty of wise statesmanship and the essential office of those in charge of the State. Now, States are made prosperous especially by wholesome morality, properly ordered family life, protection of religion and justice, moderate imposition and equitable distribution of public burdens, progressive development of industry and trade, thriving agriculture, and by all other things of this nature, which the more actively they are promoted, the better and happier the life of the citizens is destined to be. Therefore, by virtue of these things, it is within the competence of the rulers of the State that, as they benefit other groups, they also improve in particular the condition of the workers. Furthermore, they do this with full right and without laying themselves open to any charge of unwarranted interference. For the State is bound by the very law of its office to serve the common interest. And the richer the benefits which come from this general providence on the part of the State, the less necessary it will be to experiment with other measures for the well-being of workers [RERUM NOVARUM, 48].

In SUMMI PONTIFICATUS Pope Pius XII gave this directive:

. . . it is the noble prerogative and function of the State to control, aid, and direct the private and individual activities of national life that they converge harmoniously towards the common good [SUMMI PONTIFICATUS, 54].

Again, in his 1943 address, he told the Italian workers

. . . not to aim at making the lives of individuals depend entirely on the whims of the State, but to procure rather that the State, whose duty it is to promote the common good, may, through social institutions such as insurance and social-security societies, supply support and complete all that helps to strengthen workers' associations, and especially the fathers and mothers of families who are earning a livelihood for themselves and their dependents through work (Italian Workers 1943, 5).

State and Family. The duty of the State in "directing" is especially insisted on in regard to the welfare of the family. For example:

To desire, therefore, that the civil power should enter arbitrarily into the privacy of homes is a great and pernicious error. If a family perchance is in such extreme difficulty and is so completely without plans that it is entirely unable to help itself, it is right that the distress be remedied by public aid, for each individual family is a part of the community [RERUM NOVARUM, 21].

The State and politics have, in fact, precisely the office of securing for the family of every social class conditions necessary for them to exist and to evolve as economic, juridical, and moral units (Women, 715).

If, however, for this purpose, private resources do not suffice, it is the duty of the public authority to supply for the insufficient forces of individual effort, particularly in a matter which is of such importance to the common weal, touching as it does the maintenance of the family and married people. If families, particularly those in which there are many children, have not suitable dwellings; if the husband cannot find employment and means of livelihood; if the necessities of life cannot be purchased except at exorbitant prices; if even the mother of the family, to the great harm of the home, is compelled to go forth and seek a living by her own labor; if she, too, in the ordinary or even extraordinary labors of childbirth, is deprived of proper food, medicine, and the assistance of a skilled physician, it is patent to all to what an extent married people may lose heart, and how home life and the observance of God's commands are rendered difficult for them; indeed it is obvious how great a peril can arise to the public security and to the welfare and very life of civil society itself when such men are reduced to that condition of desperation that, having nothing which they fear to lose, they are emboldened to hope for chance advantage from the upheaval of the state and of established order.

Wherefore, those who have the care of the State and of the public good cannot neglect the needs of married people and their families, without bringing great harm upon the State and on the common welfare. Hence, in making the laws and disposing of public funds they must do their utmost to relieve the needs of the poor, considering such a task as one of the most important of their administrative duties [CASTI CONNUBII, pp. 43-44].

WATCHING

More Than Mere Guardian of Law. In addition to directing, the function of the State "is to watch over the community and its parts," as explained in the statement of Pope Pius XI.

With regard to civil authority, Leo XIII, boldly breaking through the confines imposed by Liberalism, fearlessly taught that government must not be thought a mere guardian of law and of good order, but rather must put forth every effort so that "through the entire scheme of laws and institutions . . . both public and individual well-being may develop spontaneously out of the very structure and administration of the State" [RERUM NOVARUM, 48]. Just freedom of action must, of course, be left both to individual citizens and to families, yet only on condition that the common good be preserved and wrong to any individual be abolished. The function of the rulers of the State, moreover, is to watch over the community and its parts; but in protecting private individuals in their rights, chief consideration ought to be given to the weak and the poor [QUADRAGESIMO ANNO, 25].

Again, in "Atheistic Communism":

In view of this organized common effort towards peaceful living, Catholic doctrine vindicates to the State the dignity and authority of a vigilant and provident defender of those divine and human rights on which the Sacred Scriptures and the Fathers of the Church insist so often [DIVINI REDEMPTORIS, 33].

In consequence, there always remains, too, his inalienable right, which no opposition can nullify—a right which must be respected by friend and foe—to a legal order and practice which appreciate and understand that it is their essential duty to serve the common good.

The juridical order has, besides, the high and difficult scope of insuring harmonious relations both between individuals and between societies, and within these (Christmas 1942, 8).

URGING

Urging, stimulating, promoting the general welfare—these also come within the purview of the State. Responsibility takes the form of promoting harmony between classes. "First and foremost, the State and every good citizen ought to look to and strive toward this end: that the conflict between the hostile classes be abolished and harmonious co-operation of the Industries and Professions be encouraged and promoted" [QUADRAGESIMO ANNO, 81]. "And the genuine and chief function of public and civil authority consists precisely in the efficacious furthering of this harmony and co-ordination of all social forces" [DIVINI REDEMPTORIS, 32].

Industry Associations. A particular and very important obligation of the government in furthering the common good takes the form of encouraging the establishment of industry associations and fostering their welfare within the limits wherein the State should act regarding them. "The social policy of the State, therefore, must devote itself to the re-establishment of the Industries and Professions" [QUADRAGESIMO ANNO, 82]. "Social charity, moreover, ought to be as the soul of this order, an order which public authority ought to be ever ready effectively to protect and defend" [QUADRAGESIMO ANNO, 88].

Pope Pius XI points up the mistake of failing in this duty and the timely advice given in RERUM NOVARUM.

And while the principles of Liberalism were tottering, which had long prevented effective action by those governing the State, the Encyclical *On the Condition of Workers* in truth impelled peoples themselves to promote a social policy on truer grounds and with greater intensity, and so strongly encouraged good Catholics to furnish valuable help to heads of States in this field that they often stood forth as illustrious champions of this new policy even in legislatures [QUADRAGESIMO ANNO, 27].

Pope Pius XII names the detailed function to be exercised by the State in relation to economic organization:

In the general framework of labor to stimulate the sane and responsible development of all the energies, physical and spiritual, of individuals in their free organization there opens up a wide field of action where the public authority comes in with its integrating and co-ordinating activity, exercised first through the local and professional corporations and finally in the activity of the State itself, whose higher moderating social authority has the important duty of forestalling the dislocations of economic balance arising from plurality and divergence of clashing interests, individual and collective (Pentecost, 3).

If Labor and Management Fail. If labor and management fail to organize because they will not or cannot, then the State has certain duties that it must fulfill toward them. Pope Pius XII specifies some of them in the following passage:

But note that such a duty and the corresponding right to work are imposed on and conceded to the individual in the first instance by nature and not by society as if man were nothing more than a mere slave or official of the community. From that it follows that the duty and the right to organize the labor of the people belong, above all, to the people immediately interested: the employers and the workers.

If they do not fulfill their functions or cannot because of special extraordinary emergencies, then it falls back on the State to intervene in the field of labor and in the division and distribution of work according to the form and measure that the common good, properly understood, demands.

In any case, every legitimate and beneficial interference of the State in the field of labor should be such as to safeguard and respect its personal character, both in the broad outlines and as far as possible in what concerns its execution; and this will happen if the norms of the State do not abolish or render impossible the exercise of other rights and duties equally personal, such as the right to give God His due worship; the right to marry; the right of husband and wife, of father and mother to lead a married domestic life; the right to reasonable liberty in the choice of a state of life and the fulfilment of a true vocation; a personal right, this last, if there ever was one, belonging to the spirit of man and sublime when the higher imprescriptible rights of God and of the Church meet, as in the choice and fulfilment of the priestly and religious vocations (Pentecost, 11-12).

The function therefore of the civil authority residing in the State is twofold, to protect and to foster, but by no means to absorb the family and the individual, or to substitute itself for them [DIVINI ILLIUS MAGISTRI, 16].

And finally, direct and indirect recognition and actualization of the inborn rights of man, which, being inherent in human nature, are always in conformity with the common interest.

Far more than that, these rights must be held to be essential elements of that common good. Whence it follows that the duty of the State is to protect and promote them. In no case may they be sacrificed to an alleged reason of State (Law, 756).

Co-ordinating Production. State activity in urging and co-ordinating is called for in the area of production also. Pope Pius XII shows why the State's exercise of its "undeniable function of co-ordination" in production is more necessary under present conditions.

. . . the duty of increasing production and of adjusting it wisely to the needs and the dignity of man brings to the fore the question of how the economy should be ordered in the field of production.

Now, although the public authorities should not substitute their oppressive omnipotence for the legitimate independence of private initiatives, these authorities have, in this matter, an undeniable function of co-ordination, which is made even more necessary by the confusion of present, and especially social, conditions.

Specifically, without the co-operation of the public authorities it is not possible to formulate an integral economic policy which would promote the active co-operation on the part of all and the increase of industrial production—direct source of national income (Semaines 1952, 12).

RESTRAINING

Function of Juridic Order. If directing, watching, and urging are not sufficient, the State in a sound social order "has also the power of coercion against those who only by this means can be held within the noble discipline of social life" as Pope Pius XII said in his 1942 Christmas message:

That social life, such as God willed it, may attain its scope, it needs a juridical order to support it from without, to defend and protect it. The function of this juridical order is not to dominate but to serve, to help the development and increase of society's vitality in the rich multiplicity of its ends, leading all the individual energies to their perfection in peaceful competition, and defending them with appropriate and honest means against all that may militate against their full evolution. Such an order, that it may safeguard the equilibrium, the safety, and harmony of society, has also the power of coercion against those who only by this means can be held within the noble discipline of social life. But in the just fulfillment of this right, an authority which is truly worthy of the name will always be painfully conscious of its responsibility in the sight of the Eternal Judge. . . .

In any case, whatever be the change or transformation, the scope of every social life remains identical, sacred, obligatory: it is the development of the personal values of man as the image of God; and the obligation remains with every member of the human family to realize his unchangeable destiny, whosoever be the legislator and the authority whom he obeys (Christmas 1942, 7).

The relations of man to man, of the individual to society, to authority, to civil duties; the relations of society and of authority to the individual, should be placed on a firm juridic footing and be guarded, when the need arises, by the authority of the courts (Christmas 1942, 18).

Pope Pius XI had expressed the same idea.

Man cannot be exempted from his divinely-imposed obligations toward civil society, and the representatives of authority have the right to coerce him when he refuses without reason to do his duty. Society, on the other hand, cannot defraud man of his God-granted rights. . . . Nor can society systematically void these rights by making their use impossible [DIVINI REDEMPTORIS, 30].

In RERUM NOVARUM, Pope Leo had likewise defended limited State intervention.

. . . those who govern must see to it that they protect the community and its constituent parts: the community, because nature has entrusted its safeguarding to the sovereign power in the State to such an extent that the protection of the public welfare is not only the supreme law, but is the entire cause and reason for sovereignty; and the constituent parts, because philosophy and Christian faith agree that the administration of the State has from nature as its purpose, not the benefit of those to whom it has been entrusted, but the benefit of those who have been entrusted to it. And since the power of governing comes from God and is a participation, as it were, in His supreme sovereignty, it ought to be administered according to the example of the Divine power, which looks with paternal care to the welfare of individual creatures as well as to that of all creation. If, therefore, any injury has been done to or threatens either the common good or the interests of individual groups, which injury cannot in any other way be repaired or prevented, it is necessary for public authority to intervene [RERUM NOVARUM, 52].

Defender of All. In exercising its power of "restraining," the State must be the defender of all, but especially of the poor and wage earners.

Rights indeed, by whomsoever possessed, must be religiously protected; and public authority, in warding off injuries and punishing wrongs, ought to see to it that individuals may have and hold what belongs to them. In protecting the rights of private individuals, however, special consideration must be given to the weak and the poor. For the nation, as it were, of the rich, is guarded by its own defences and is in less need of governmental protection, whereas the suffering multitude, without the means to protect itself, relies especially on the protection of the State. Wherefore, since wage workers are numbered among the great mass of the needy, the State must include them under its special care and foresight [RERUM NOVARUM, 54].

And to accomplish this purpose [protection of the interests of the workers] she holds that the laws and the authority of the State, within reasonable limits, ought to be employed [RERUM NOVARUM, 25].

This ought to be considered, as it touches the question more deeply, namely, that the State has one basic purpose for existence, which embraces in common the highest and the lowest of its members. Non-owning workers are unquestionably citizens by nature in virtue of the same right as the rich, that is, true and vital parts whence, through the medium of families, the body of the State is constituted; and it hardly need be added that they are by far the greatest number in every urban area. Since it would be quite absurd to look out for one portion of the citizens and to neglect another, it follows that public authority ought to exercise due care in safeguarding the well-being and the interests of non-owning workers. Unless this is done, justice, which commands that everyone be given his own, will be violated. Wherefore St. Thomas says wisely: "Even as part and whole are in a certain way the same, so too that which pertains to the whole pertains in a certain way to the part also." Consequently, among the numerous and weighty duties of rulers who would serve their people well, this is first and foremost, namely, that they protect equitably each and every class of citizens, maintaining inviolate that justice especially which is called *distributive* [RERUM NOVARUM, 49].

Nevertheless, an abundance of corporeal and external goods is likewise a characteristic of a well-constituted State, "the use of which goods is necessary for the practice of virtue." To produce these goods the labor of the workers, whether they expend their skill and strength on farms or in factories, is most efficacious and necessary. Nay, in this respect, their energy and effectiveness are so important that it is incontestable that the wealth of nations originates from no other source than from the labor of workers. Equity therefore commands that public authority show proper concern for the worker so that from what he contributes to the common good he may receive what will enable him, housed, clothed, and secure, to live his life without hardship. Whence, it follows that all those measures ought to be favored which seem in any way capable of benefiting the condition of workers. Such solicitude is so far from injuring anyone that it is destined rather to benefit all, because it is of absolute interest to the State that those citizens should not be miserable in every respect from whom such necessary goods proceed [RERUM NOVARUM, 51].

Pope Pius XI detailed the various laws which had been passed to protect the workers.

A new branch of law, wholly unknown to the earlier time, has arisen from this continuous and unwearied labor to protect vigorously the sacred rights of the workers that flow from their dignity as men and as Christians. These laws undertake the protection of life, health, strength, family, homes, workshops, wages, and labor hazards, in fine, everything which pertains to the condition of wage workers, with special concern for women and children. Even though these laws do not conform exactly everywhere and in all respects to Leo's recommendations, still it is undeniable that much in them savors of the Encyclical, *On the Condition of Workers,* to which great credit must be given for whatever improvement has been achieved in the workers' condition [QUADRAGESIMO ANNO, 28].

Regulate Competition. Finally, regulation of competition also comes within the scope of the "restraining" power of the State. "Free competition, kept within definite and due limits, and still more economic dictatorship, must be effectively brought under public authority in these matters which pertain to the latter's function" [QUADRAGESIMO ANNO, 110].

This power, however, should not be exercised in an unlimited manner and in violation of the Christian conception of social economy.

There are even countries where a policy has been adopted, more or less absolute, that places all commerce in the hands of public authority. Let us affirm this clearly: this is a tendency in opposition to the Christian conception of social economy. Commerce is fundamentally an activity of the individual and it is this private activity that gives a man his first impulse and lights the flame of his enthusiasm (Businessmen, 510).

The foregoing principles, clarified by the Sovereign Pontiffs both by definition and application, furnish a foundation upon which the Industry Council Plan attempts to form an organic society based upon the dignity of the human persons who compose it.

Part Three

Social Principles Which Indirectly Refer to the Industry Council Plan

Chapter XI

Position of the Church;
Position of the State

POSITION OF THE CHURCH

To CLARIFY OUR THINKING and to safeguard ourselves against unwarranted assumptions it is necessary to note the position which the Church, in the person of the Popes, occupies—the basis for its action in economic matters and the extent and limitations of its role.

Authority to Speak on Economics. First, what is the basis and authority of the Church for its action in economic matters?

Yet before proceeding to explain these matters, that principle which Leo XIII so clearly established must be laid down at the outset here, namely, that there resides in Us the right

*For a complete understanding of the papal position on the principles involved in the Industry Council Plan, it is necessary to be aware of certain social principles which are indirectly related to the Plan. In the following chapters, in which ten such areas are discussed, it has been difficult to arrange a "logical" order or sequence. The aim has been rather to group those principles which have similar applications. The ten areas are the position of the Church, the position of the State, man and society, social justice, moral reform, the use of material goods, private property, dignity of labor, the family, and international order.

and duty to pronounce with supreme authority upon social and economic matters [QUADRAGESIMO ANNO, 41].

Since a problem was being treated "for which no satisfactory solution" is found "unless religion and the Church have been called upon to aid" [RERUM NOVARUM, 24], the Pope, clearly exercising his right and correctly holding that the guardianship of religion and the stewardship over those things that are closely bound up with it had been entrusted especially to him and relying solely upon the unchangeable principles drawn from the treasury of right reason and Divine Revelation, confidently and *as one having authority* (Matt. 7:29), declared and proclaimed "the rights and duties within which the rich and the proletariat—those who furnish material things and those who furnish work—ought to be restricted in relation to each other" [RERUM NOVARUM, 4], and what the Church, heads of States and the people themselves directly concerned ought to do [QUADRAGESIMO ANNO, 11].

In keeping with the responsibility of the Church to uphold the moral law and further its observance she has taken the lead in working for a correct social order.

1. No one can accuse the Church of having disregarded the workers and the social question, or of not having given them and it their due importance.

Few questions have occupied the Church so much as these two from the day when, sixty years ago [the Pope is writing in 1951], Our great predecessor Leo XIII, with his encyclical, RERUM NOVARUM, put into the hands of the workers the Magna Carta of their rights.

.   .   .   .

She has offered for her part wide and well-planned programs for the religious-moral arrangement of all the social order. The social legislation of the different countries is, for the greater part, no more than the application of the principles established by the Church.

Do not forget either that all that is good and just in other systems is already in Catholic social doctrine.

And when goals which the Church rejects are ascribed to the workers' movement, these always concern illusory objectives which sacrifice truth, human dignity, and the genuine welfare of all the citizens.

2. In its 2,000-year history the Church has had to live in the midst of the most diverse social structures, from the ancient one with its slavery to the modern economic system marked by the words capitalism and proletariat. The Church has never preached social revolution; but always and everywhere, from the Epistle of St. Paul to Philemon to the social teachings of the Popes of the nineteenth and twentieth centuries, she has worked hard to have more concern shown for the human being than for economic and technical advantages, and to get as many as possible, on their part, to do all they can to live a Christian life and one worthy of a human being (Spanish Employers and Workers, 706-707).

Secondly, in what area does the Church disclaim jurisdiction?

The Church has been and is always fully conscious of her responsibility. Without the Church the social question is insoluble. But neither can she solve it alone. She needs the collaboration of the intellectual, economic and technical resources of leaders in public life (Spanish Employers and Workers, 706).

He [Leo XIII] had no intention of laying down guiding principles of the purely practical, we might say the technical side of the social structure; for he was well aware of the fact—as Our immediate predecessor of saintly memory, Pius XI, pointed out ten years ago [i.e., in 1931] in his commemorative Encyclical, QUADRAGESIMO ANNO—that the Church does not claim such a mission (Pentecost, 3).

Indeed "the Church holds that it is unlawful for her to mix without cause in these temporal concerns," however, she can in no wise renounce the duty God entrusted to her to interpose her authority, not of course in matters of technique for which she is neither suitably equipped nor endowed by office, but in all things that are connected with the moral law [QUADRAGESIMO ANNO, 41].

Technical Problems. The Church leaves the solution of the technical problems to social scientists and to the practical men in the field. To them was the exhortation of Pope Pius XII addressed when he said:

In the domain of social economy the duty pressing for attention is the judicious adjustment of production to consumption on the basis of human needs and human dignity. In view of this urgency, the question which comes to the fore today is that of the organization and equipment of the social economy at its production stage. The solution of this question must not be sought from the theory of "laws of the market"—a purely positivistic by-product of neo-Kantian criticism—nor in the mere formula, every bit as artificial, of "full employment." There before you is the problem on which We should like to see the theorists and practical men of the Catholic social movement concentrate their attention and bring their studies to bear (Production, 509-510).

To achieve this latter lofty aim [initiation of a better social order], and in particular to promote the common good truly and permanently, We hold it is first and above everything wholly necessary that God bless it and, secondly, that all men of good will work with united effort toward that end.

We are further convinced, as a necessary consequence, that this end will be attained the more certainly the larger the number of those ready to contribute toward it their technical, occupational, and social knowledge and experience. . . . [QUAD-RAGESIMO ANNO, 96].

POSITION OF THE STATE
IN MODERN SOCIETY

Right to Rule from God. Several of the Pontiffs para-phrase the thought from *Diuturnum Illud:* ". . . the right to rule is from God, as from a natural and necessary princi-ple" [DIUTURNUM ILLUD, 5].

But no man has in himself or of himself the power of con-straining the free will of others by fetters of authority of this kind. This power resides solely in God, the Creator and legis-lator of all things; and it is necessary that those who exercise it should do it as having received it from God [DIUTURNUM ILLUD, 11].

It is of importance, however, to remark in this place that those who may be placed over the State may in certain cases be chosen by the will and decision of the multitude, without opposition to or impugning of the Catholic doctrine. And by this choice, in truth, the ruler is designated, but the rights of ruling are not thereby conferred. Nor is the authority delegated to him, but the person by whom it is to be exercised is deter-mined upon [DIUTURNUM ILLUD, 6].

Hence it follows that all public power must proceed from God. For God alone is the true and supreme Lord of the world. Everything, without exception, must be subject to Him, and must serve Him, so that whosoever holds the right to govern, holds it from one sole and single source, namely, God, the Sovereign Ruler of all. There is no power but from God (Rom. xiii, 1) [IMMORTALE DEI, 3].

Again:

Law is but the order of right reason, proceeding from lawful authority for the common good. There is no true and lawful authority except that which comes from God, the sovereign Lord of all, who alone has power to give man authority over his fellow man. There is no right reason which is contrary to truth and to the law of God; and no true good which does not accord with the highest imperishable good . . . [SAPIENTIAE CHRISTIANAE, 3].

Pope Pius XII states the same principle:

. . . all legitimate power over men has its source and being only in the authority of Him Who possesses it by nature, in Heaven and on earth, without limit of time or space, namely, Jesus Christ, Who rules over the powerful of this world . . . (Labor's Dignity, 305).

Purpose of the State. The purpose of the State is to promote the common temporal welfare in order that man may attain the perfection of his nature.

These rights have been conferred upon civil society by the Author of nature Himself . . . in virtue of the authority which it possesses to promote the common temporal welfare, which is precisely the purpose of its existence. . . .

Now this end and object, the common welfare in the temporal order, consists in that peace and security in which families and individual citizens have the free exercise of their rights, and at the same time enjoy the greatest spiritual and temporal prosperity possible in this life, by the mutual union and co-ordination of the work of all [DIVINI ILLIUS MAGISTRI, p. 16].

. . . in its nature, it [civil power] is constituted to provide for the common good, the supreme end which gives human society its origin . . . this good is, after God, the first and last law in society [AU MILIEU DES SOLLICITUDES, pp. 257-258].

. . . the State as guardian of the law, which, like society in general itself, has its proximate origin and its end in the complete man, in the human person, the image of God (Society, 200).

As human experience teaches them, the state and the society of states with its external organization, in spite of all their defects, are naturally, given the social nature of man, forms of union and order among men; they are necessary for human life; they contribute to its perfection (Christmas 1951, 252).

Test of Good Government. From this it follows that the test of good government consists in evaluating the degree to which it fulfills the common good. How this common good is to be determined is explained by Pope Leo XIII: "In political affairs, and all matters civil, the laws aim at securing the common good, and are not framed according to the delusive caprices and opinions of the mass of the people, but by truth and by justice; the ruling powers are invested with a sacredness more than human . . ." [IMMORTALE DEI, 18]. Further, no particular type of government is declared necessary provided the correct principles are observed. Government "may take this or that form, provided only that it be of a nature to insure the general welfare" [IMMORTALE DEI, 4]. ". . . provided only it be just, and that it tend to the common advantage. Wherefore, *so long as justice be respected, the people are not hindered from choosing for themselves that form of government which suits best either their own disposition, or the institutions and customs of their ancestors*" [DIUTURNUM ILLUD, 7].

In this order of speculative ideas, Catholics, like other citizens, are free to prefer one form of government to another precisely because no one of these social forms is, in itself, opposed to the principles of sound reason nor to the maxims of Christian doctrine [AU MILIEU DES SOLLICITUDES, 225].

God Is Ruler of World. Rulers are merely instruments; they must recognize that "God is the paramount ruler of the world."

But whatever be the nature of the government, rulers must ever bear in mind that God is the paramount ruler of the world, and must set Him before themselves as their exemplar and law in the administration of the State. For, in things visible, God has fashioned secondary causes, in which His divine action can in some wise be discerned, leading up to the end to which the course of the world is ever tending. In like manner in civil society, God has always willed that there should be a ruling authority, and that they who are invested with it should reflect the divine power and providence in some measure over the human race [IMMORTALE DEI, 4].

. . . it was the Creator's will that civil sovereignty should regulate social life after the dictates of an order changeless in its universal principles; should facilitate the attainment in the temporal order, by individuals, of physical, intellectual, and moral perfection; and should aid them to reach their supernatural end [SUMMI PONTIFICATUS, 53].

It is only within this framework that those in power can properly fulfill their duties.

Only a clear appreciation of the purposes assigned by God to every human society, joined to a deep sense of the exalted duties of social activity, can put those in power in a position to fulfill their own obligations in the legislative, judicial, and executive order with that objectivity, impartiality, loyalty, generosity, and integrity without which a democratic government would find it hard to command the respect and the support of the better section of the people.

The deep sense of the principles underlying a political and social order that is sound and conforms to the norms of right and justice is of special importance in those who in any kind of democratic regime have, as the people's delegates, in whole or part, the power to legislate (Christmas 1944, 70).

Return to Ethics Needed. To achieve this social responsibility, a return to an ethical conception of law is necessary.

[One] will realize at once the urgent need of a return to a conception of law which is spiritual and ethical, serious and profound, vivified by the warmth of true humanity and illumined by the splendor of the Christian Faith, which bids us seek in the juridical order an outward refraction of the social order willed by God, a luminous product of the spirit of man which is in turn the image of the Spirit of God (Christmas 1942, 9).

Pope Pius XII warns that the well-being of nations and the prosperity of human society are harmed by the error of divorcing "civil authority from every kind of dependence upon the Supreme Being—First Source and absolute Master of man and of society—and from every restraint of a Higher Law derived from God as from its First Source" [summi pontificatus, 47]. Pope Pius XI writes in the same vein.

> He who takes . . . the State, or the form of Government, the bearers of the power of the State or other fundamental elements of human society—which in the temporal order of things have an essential and honorable place—out of the system of their earthly valuation, and makes them the ultimate norm of all, even of religious values, and deifies them with an idolatrous worship, perverts and falsifies the order of things created and commanded by God [mit brennender sorge, 12].

Violation of God's Order. The Pope, in his message to President Truman, traces the consequences flowing from the violation of this order established by God.

> It was He Who of necessity assigned man's purpose in life. It is from Him, with consequent necessity, that man derives personal imprescriptible rights to pursue that purpose and to be unhindered in the attainment of it. Civic society is also of Divine origin and indicated by nature itself but it is subsequent to man and meant to be a means to defend him and to help him in the legitimate exercise of his God-given rights. Once the state to the exclusion of God makes itself the source of the rights of the human person, man is forthwith reduced to the condition of a slave or a mere civic commodity to be exploited for the selfish aims of a group that happens to have power. The order of God is overturned and history surely makes it clear to those who wish to read that the inevitable result of the subversion of order between peoples is war (Truman, 654).

> Whether this slavery [which violates the rights of man as a person] arises from the exploitation of private capital or from

the power of the state, the result is the same. Indeed, under the pressure of a state which dominates all and controls the whole field of public and private life, even going into the realm of ideas and beliefs and of conscience, this lack of liberty can have the more serious consequences, as experience shows and proves (Christmas 1942, 12).

Men have fallen away miserably from Jesus Christ, falling from their first happiness into a slough of misery, and that is the reason for the failure of all they do to repair the ills and save something from the wreck. God and the Lord Christ have been removed from the conduct of public affairs, authority is now derived not from God but from men, and it has come about—in addition to the fact that the laws lack the true and sound sanctions and the supreme principles of justice which even pagan philosophers like Cicero recognized must be sought in the eternal law of God—that the very foundations of authority have been swept away by removing the primary reason by which some have the right of rule, others the duty of obedience. Hence came inevitably the shock to the whole community of society, no longer supported by any solid safeguarding stay, with nothing left but factions fighting for command among themselves and for their own benefit, not for the country's good [UBI ARCANO DEI, pp. 303-304].

Pope Pius also deplores the perverted use of State intervention in direct violation of these principles. He says that

To these are to be added the grave evils that have resulted from an intermingling and shameful confusion of the functions and duties of public authority with those of the economic sphere—such as, one of the worst, the virtual degradation of the majesty of the State, which although it ought to sit on high like a queen and supreme arbitress, free from all partiality and intent upon the one common good and justice, is become a slave, surrendered and delivered to the passions and greed of men. And as to international relations, two different streams have issued from the one fountain-head: On the one hand, economic nationalism or even economic imperialism; on the other, a no less deadly and accursed internationalism of finance or international imperialism whose country is where profit is [QUADRAGESIMO ANNO, 109].

Duties of Citizens. In his Easter message of 1939, the Pope indicates what is involved in the mutual relationship between man and the State. "Now justice requires that to lawfully constituted authority there be given that respect and obedience which is its due; that the laws which are made shall be in wise conformity with common good; and that, as a matter of conscience, all men shall render obedience to these laws" (Easter, 130). He is echoing Pope Leo XIII, who had said ". . . they must be persuaded that they who resist State authority resist the divine Will; that they who refuse honor to rulers refuse it to God Himself" [DIUTURNUM ILLUD, 13]. Laws are to be obeyed, however, "only in so far as they conform with right reason and thus with the eternal law of God" [RERUM NOVARUM, 72].

Masses vs. People. Pope Pius XII shows that "the masses" and "the people" are two very different concepts and that the dynamic character of the State in its function of promoting the general welfare or common good among the people should be a unifying factor in organic society, preventing the people from degenerating into "the masses." The passage reads as follows:

The State does not contain in itself and does not mechanically bring together in a given territory a shapeless mass of individuals.

It is and should be in practice the organic and organizing unity of a real people. The people and a shapeless multitude (or as it is called "the masses") are two distinct concepts.

The people lives and moves by its own life energy; the masses are inert of themselves and can only be moved from outside. The people lives by the fulness of life in the men that compose it, each of them at his proper place and in his own responsibility and of his own views.

The masses, on the contrary, wait for the impulse from outside, an easy plaything in the hands of anyone who exploits their instincts and impressions; ready to follow, in turn, today this flag, tomorrow another.

From the exuberant life of a true people, an abundant rich life is diffused in the state and all its organs, instilling into them, with a vigor that is always renewing itself, the consciousness of their own responsibility, the true instinct for the common good.

The elementary power of the masses, deftly managed and employed, the State also can utilize. In the ambitious hands of one or of several who have been artificially brought together for selfish aims, the State itself, with the support of the masses, reduced to the minimum status of a mere machine, can impose its whims on the better part of the real people, the common interest remains seriously and for a long time injured by this process, and the injury is very often hard to heal.

Hence follows clearly another conclusion: the masses—as we have just defined them—are the capital enemy of true democracy and of its ideal of liberty and equality.

In a people worthy of the name the citizen feels within him the consciousness of his personality, of his duties and rights, of his own freedom joined to respect for the freedom and dignity of others (Christmas 1944, 68).

Legislators. Legislators should look on themselves as the representatives of the entire populace and not as "the mandatories of a mob":

To secure effective action, to win esteem and trust, every legislative body should—as experience shows beyond doubt—gather within it a group of select men, spiritually eminent and of strong character, who shall look upon themselves as the representatives of the entire people and not the mandatories of a mob, whose interests are often unfortunately made to prevail over the true needs of the common good—a select group of men not restricted to any profession or social standing but reflecting every phase of the people's life; men chosen for their solid Christian convictions, straight and steady judgment, with a sense of the practical and equitable, true to themselves in all circumstances; men of clear and sound principles, with sound and clear-cut proposals to make; men, above all, capable, in virtue of the authority that emanates from their untarnished consciences and radiates widely from them, to be leaders and heads especially in times when the pressing needs of the moment excite the people's impressionability unduly and render it more liable to be led astray and get lost; men who in periods of transition, generally stormy and disturbed by passion, by divergent opinions and opposing programs, feel themselves doubly under the obligation to send circulating through the veins of the people and of the State, burning with a thousand fevers, the spiritual antidote of clear views, kindly interest, a justice equally sympathetic to all and a bias toward national unity and concord in a sincere spirit of brotherhood (Christmas 1944, 70-71).

The Executive. The executive must constantly keep in mind the common good; government must not be administered for the advantage of the few.

The State itself, mindful of its responsibility before God and society, should be a model of prudence and sobriety in the administration of the commonwealth. Today more than ever the acute world crisis demands that those who dispose of immense funds, built upon the sweat and toil of millions, keep constantly and singly in mind the common good. State functionaries and all employees are obliged in conscience to perform their duties faithfully and unselfishly, imitating the brilliant example of distinguished men of the past and of our own day, who with unremitting labor sacrificed their all for the good of their country [DIVINI REDEMPTORIS, 76].

Pope Leo warns us that the interests of the government must be for all and not for certain individuals only.

Government should, moreover, be administered for the well-being of the citizens because they who govern others possess authority solely for the welfare of the State. Furthermore, the civil power must not be subservient to the advantage of any one individual or of some few persons, inasmuch as it was established for the common good of all [IMMORTALE DEI, 5].

But in order that justice may be retained in government it is of the highest importance that those who rule states should understand that political power was not created for the advantage of any private individual; and that the administration of the State must be carried on to the profit of those who have been committed to their care, not to the profit of those to whom it has been committed [DIUTURNUM ILLUD, 16].

State Ownership. State ownership can be justified under certain conditions and in certain areas; but it is not "the normal rule for public economic organization." Licit State ownership is thus defined: "For certain kinds of property, it is rightly contended, ought to be reserved to the State since they carry with them a dominating power so great that it cannot without danger to the general welfare be entrusted to private individuals" [QUADRAGESIMO ANNO, 114]. This is not a surrender to Socialism for "such just demands and desires have nothing in them now which is inconsistent with Christian truth, and much less are they special to Socialism. Those who work solely toward such ends have, therefore, no reason to become socialists" [QUADRAGESIMO ANNO, 115].

So also the war declared on private ownership, more and more abated, is being so restricted that now, finally, not the possession itself of the means of production is attacked but rather a kind of sovereignty over society which ownership has, contrary to all right, seized and usurped. For such sovereignty belongs in reality not to owners, but to the public authority [QUADRAGESIMO ANNO, 114].

Limitations on State Ownership. But we must keep in mind a limitation in this area also, as both Popes Pius XI and Pius XII remind us.

There can be no question that the Church also admits—within certain just limits—state ownership and management, judging that "certain forms of property may legitimately be reserved to the public authority: those which represent a dominating power so great that it cannot without danger to the general welfare be entrusted to private individuals" [QUADRAGESIMO ANNO]. But to make of this state enterprise the normal rule for public economic organization would mean reversing the order of things. Actually it is the mission of public law to serve private rights, not to absorb them. The economy is not of its nature—not more, for that matter, than any other human activity—a state institution. It is, on the contrary, the living product of the free initiative of individuals and of their freely established associations (Employers, 446-447).

The Catholic social principles support nationalization only in cases where it appears really necessary for the common welfare; in other words, when it is the only means to remedy an injustice and to ensure the co-ordinated use of the same forces to the benefit of the economic life of the nation, so that the normal and peaceful development of that economic life may open the gates to material prosperity for all, a prosperity which may become a sound foundation for the development of cultural and religious life. In any case, the Associations recognize that nationalization carries with it the obligation of fitting compensation, such as in concrete circumstances is just and fair to those concerned.

Chapter XII

Man and Society;
Social Justice; Moral Reform

AFTER HAVING TRACED the responsibility and authority of the Church and State in modern society, a consideration of the nature of man, of society, and the relationship existing between the two is in order. Then we can take up the duty that all have in social justice to help in the reorganization of society and end the chapter with another essential of reorganization—moral reform.

MAN AND SOCIETY

Dignity of the Human Person. In speaking to Catholic jurists Pope Pius XII describes the nature of man after being invested with supernatural life.

In the new economy man is not in a state of pure nature, but man has been elevated through grace by the Saviour to a supernatural order, and by this fact itself man has been put in contact with divinity by means of new life, which is the very life of God, even though it is only shared. Man's dignity increases, therefore, by infinite proportions. . . . (Jurists, 56).

116

Resultant Rights. Pope Pius XI reminds us, "that we should be called and should be the sons of God" (I John iii. 1) [MIT BRENNENDER SORGE, 33]. Thus the true dignity of man consists in this: "Man is the image of the Triune God and is therefore himself a person, brother of the Man-God Jesus Christ, and with Him and through Him heir to a life eternal: that is where his true dignity lies (Labor's Dignity, 303). This dignity results in rights.

In the Encyclical on Christian Education We explained the fundamental doctrine concerning man as it may be gathered from reason and Faith. Man has a spiritual and immortal soul. He is a person, marvelously endowed by his Creator with gifts of body and mind. He is a true "microcosm," as the ancients said, a world in miniature, with a value far surpassing that of the vast inanimate cosmos. God alone is his last end, in this life and the next. By sanctifying grace he is raised to the dignity of a son of God, and incorporated into the Kingdom of God in the Mystical Body of Christ. In consequence he has been endowed by God with many and varied prerogatives: the right to life, to bodily integrity, to the necessary means of existence; the right to tend toward his ultimate goal in the path marked out for him by God; the right of association and the right to possess and use property [DIVINI REDEMPTORIS, 27].

The dignity of the human person, then, requires normally as a natural foundation of life the right to the use of the goods of the earth. (Christmas 1942, 12).

Workers are not to be treated as slaves; justice demands that the dignity of human personality be respected in them, ennobled as it has been through what we call the Christian character. If we hearken to natural reason and to Christian philosophy, gainful occupations are not a mark of shame to man, but rather of respect, as they provide him with an honorable means of supporting life [RERUM NOVARUM, 31].

Society. What is society?

. . . he should strive to understand society as an intrinsic unity, which has grown up and matured under the guidance of Providence, a unity which—within the bounds assigned to it and according to its own peculiar gifts—tends, with the collaboration of the various classes and professions, towards the eternal and ever new aims of culture and religion (Christmas 1942, 16).

What is its purpose? In explaining the purpose of society, Pope Pius XI reveals the error of extremes both in the direction of collectivism, which subordinates man to society, and of individualism, which subordinates society to selfish individual aims. These two extremes have been followed through a misunderstanding of the purpose of society.

But God has likewise destined man for civil society according to the dictates of his very nature. In the plan of the Creator, society is a natural means which man can and must use to reach his destined end. Society is for man and not vice versa. This must not be understood in the sense of liberalistic individualism, which subordinates society to the selfish use of the individual; but only in the sense that by means of an organic union with society and by mutual collaboration the attainment of earthly happiness is placed within the reach of all. In a further sense, it is society which affords the opportunities for the development of all the individual and social gifts bestowed on human nature. These natural gifts have a value surpassing the immediate interests of the moment, for in society they reflect the divine perfection, which would not be true were man to live alone. But on final analysis, even in this latter function, society is made for man, that he may recognize this reflection of God's perfection, and refer it in praise and adoration to the Creator. Only man, the human person, and not society in any form is endowed with reason and a morally free will [DIVINI REDEMPTORIS, 29].

For, according to Christian teaching, man, endowed with a social nature, is placed on this earth so that by leading a life in society and under an authority ordained of God (Cf. Rom. 13:1) he may fully cultivate and develop all his faculties unto the praise and glory of his Creator; and that by faithfully fulfilling the duties of his craft or other calling he may obtain for himself temporal and at the same time eternal happiness [QUADRAGESIMO ANNO, 118].

The community is the great means intended by nature and God to regulate the exchange of mutual needs and to aid each man to develop his personality fully according to his individual and social abilities. Considered as a whole, the community is not a physical unity subsisting in itself and its individual members are not integral parts of it (Medical Congress, 8).

Economic society should contribute to this end by furthering the temporal common good by making resources available to all.

The purpose of the economic and social organism, as we must recall, is to obtain for its members and their families all the good that the resources of nature and of industry, as well as a social organization of economic life, are capable of obtaining for them (Semaines 1952, 12).

Inter-relationship. Society is necessary for man.

Man's natural instinct moves him to live in civil society, for he cannot, if dwelling apart, provide himself with the necessary requirements of life, nor procure the means of developing his mental and moral faculties. Hence it is divinely ordained that he should lead his life—be it family, social, or civil—with his fellow men, amongst whom alone his several wants can be adequately supplied . . . no society can hold together unless someone be over all, directing all to strive earnestly for the common good . . . [IMMORTALE DEI, 3].

In viewing this dependence of man on society it must be remembered that society exists for man, not man for society.

It must be noted that, in his personal being, man is not finally ordered to usefulness to society. On the contrary, the community exists for man (Medical Congress, 8).

. . . the individual himself, who, so far from being the object and, as it were, a merely passive element in the social order, is, in fact, and must be and continue to be, its subject, its foundation, and its end (Christmas 1944, 67).

This man the Church forms and educates because he alone, complete in harmonious combination of his natural and supernatural life, in an orderly development of his instincts and inclinations, his rich qualities and varied reactions, is at the same time the beginning and the end of life in human society, thus also the principle of its equilibrium.

That is why the Apostle of the Gentiles, speaking of Christians, proclaims they are no more "children tossed to and fro" by the uncertain drift in the midst of human society (Society, 196).

Man's need for society calls for order under rule.

And indeed nature, or rather God Who is the author of nature, wills that man should live in a civil society; and this is clearly shown both by the faculty of language, the greatest medium of intercourse, and by numerous innate desires of the mind, and the many necessary things, and things of great importance, which men isolated cannot procure, but which they can procure when joined and associated with others. But now, a society can neither exist nor be conceived in which there is no one to govern the wills of individuals, in such a way as to make, as it were, one will out of many, and to impel them rightly and orderly to the common good; therefore God has willed that in a civil society there should be some to rule the multitude [DIUTURNUM ILLUD, 11].

Two primary elements, then, regulate social life: a living together in order and a living together in tranquillity.

Order, which is fundamental in an association of men (of beings, that is, who strive to attain an end appropriate to their nature), is not a merely external linking up of parts which are numerically distinct. It is rather, and must be, a tendency and an ever more perfect approach to an internal union; and this does not exclude differences founded in fact and sanctioned by the will of God or by supernatural standard.

A clear understanding of the genuine fundamentals of all social life has a capital importance today as never before, when mankind, impregnated by the poison of error and social aberrations, tormented by the fever of discordant desires, doctrines, and aims, is excitedly tossing about in the disorder which it has itself created, and is experiencing the destructive force of false ideas, that disregard the Law of God or are opposed to it. And since disorder can only be overcome by an order which is not merely superimposed and fictitious (just as darkness with its fearful and depressing effects can only be driven away by light and not by will o' the wisps); so security, reorganization, progressive improvement cannot be expected and cannot be brought about unless by a return of large and influential sections to correct notions about society.

It is a return which calls for the Grace of God in large measure, and for a resolute will, ready and prepared for sacrifice on the part of good and farseeing men (Christmas 1942, 3-4).

Means to Live This Unity. What must we do so as to live this unity of mankind?

Yet, if they obey Christian teachings, not merely friendship but brotherly love also will bind them to each other. They will feel and understand that all men indeed have been created by God, their common Father; that all strive for the same object of good, which is God Himself, Who alone can communicate to both men and angels perfect and absolute happiness; that all equally have been redeemed by the grace of Jesus Christ and restored to the dignity of the sons of God, so that they are clearly united by the bonds of brotherhood not only with one another but also with Christ the Lord, "the firstborn among many brethren," and further, that the goods of nature and the gifts of divine grace belong in common and without distinction to all human kind, and that no one, unless he is unworthy, will be deprived of the inheritance of Heaven. "But if we are sons, we are also heirs: heirs indeed of God and joint heirs with Christ" (Rom. 8:17) [RERUM NOVARUM, 38].

Both men and civil society derive their origin from the Creator, who has mutually ordained them one to the other. Hence neither can be exempted from their correlative obligations, nor deny or diminish each other's rights. The Creator Himself has regulated this mutual relationship in its fundamental lines . . . [DIVINI REDEMPTORIS, 33].

But in effecting all this, the law of charity, "which is the bond of perfection" (Col. 3:14), must always take a leading role. How completely deceived, therefore, are those rash reformers who concern themselves with the enforcement of justice alone—and this, commutative justice—and in their pride reject the assistance of charity! Admittedly, no vicarious charity can substitute for justice which is due as an obligation and is wrongfully denied. Yet even supposing that everyone should finally receive all that is due him, the widest field for charity will always remain open. For justice alone can, if faithfully observed, remove the causes of social conflict but can never bring about union of minds and hearts. Indeed all the institutions for the establishment of peace and the promotion of mutual help among men, however perfect these may seem, have the principal foundation of their stability in the mutual bond of minds and hearts whereby the members are united with one another. If this bond is lacking, the best of regulations come to naught, as we have learned by too frequent experience. And so, then only will true co-operation be possible for a single common good when the constituent parts of society deeply feel themselves members of one great family and children of the same Heavenly Father; nay, that they are one body in Christ, "but severally members one of another" (Rom. 12:5), so that "if one member suffers anything, all the members suffer with it" (I Cor. 12:26). For then the rich and others in positions of power will change their former indifference toward their poorer brothers into a solicitous and active love, listen with kindliness to their just demands, and freely forgive their possible mistakes and faults. And the workers, sincerely putting aside every feeling of hatred or envy which the promoters of social conflict so cunningly exploit, will not only accept without rancor the place in human society assigned them by Divine Providence, but rather will hold it in esteem, knowing well that everyone according to his function and duty is toiling usefully and honorably for the common good and is following closely in the footsteps of Him Who, being in the form of God, willed to be a carpenter among men and be known as the son of a carpenter [QUADRAGESIMO ANNO, 137].

The Church acts to correct the violation of this true relationship "by having access to the innermost sanctuary of the human being and placing him at the center of the whole social order. Now this human being is not man in the abstract, nor considered only in the order of pure nature, but the complete man as he is in the sight of God, His Creator and Redeemer, as he is in his concrete and historical reality, which could not be lost sight of without compromising the normal functioning of human intercourse" (Society, 197).

Finally, Pope Pius XII chants a veritable litany of unity which is "the strongest possible bond of union."

A marvelous vision, which makes us see the human race in the unity of one common origin in God "One God and Father of all, Who is above all, and through all, and in us all" (Ephesians iv: 6); in the unity of nature which in every man is equally composed of material body and spiritual, immortal soul; in the unity of the immediate end and mission in the world; in the unity of dwelling place, the earth, of whose resources all men can by natural right avail themselves, to sustain and develop life; in the unity of the supernatural end, God Himself, to Whom all should tend; in the unity of means to secure that end.

It is the same Apostle who portrays for us mankind in the unity of its relations with the Son of God, image of the invisible God, in Whom all things have been created: "in him were all things created" (Colossians i:16); in the unity of its ransom, effected for all by Christ, Who, through His holy and most bitter Passion, restored the original friendship with God which had been broken, making Himself the Mediator between God and men: "For there is one God, and one mediator of God and men, the man Christ Jesus" (I Timothy ii:5).

And to render such friendship between God and mankind more intimate, this same Divine and universal Mediator of salvation and of peace, in the sacred silence of the Supper Room, before He consummated the Supreme Sacrifice, let fall from His Divine Lips the words which reverberate mightily down the centuries, inspiring heroic charity in a world devoid of love and torn by hate: "This is my commandment, that you love one another, as I have loved you" (St. John xv:12).

These are supernatural truths which form a solid basis and the strongest possible bond of a union, that is reinforced by the love of God and of our Divine Redeemer, from Whom all receive salvation "for the edifying of the body of Christ: Until we all meet into the unity of faith, and of the knowledge of the Son of God, unto a perfect man, unto the measure of the age of the fulness of Christ" (Ephesians iv: 12, 13).

In the light of this unity of all mankind, which exists in law and in fact, individuals do not feel themselves isolated units, like grains of sand, but united by the very force of their nature and by their internal destiny, into an organic, harmonious mutual relationship which varies with the changing of times [SUMMI PONTIFICATUS, 35-37].

For further pertinent statements see Chapter IX, "General Welfare," supra, pp. 74 ff.

Applied to Industry Councils. Organization based on this intimate union existing among men in society is the natural foundation upon which we must build the system of Industry Councils. Our Holy Father in his address to the delegates to the International Labor Organization comments thus in view of the real nature of man:

We are sure that you . . . will agree that any organization for improving the condition of the workingman will be a mechanism without soul and hence without life and fecundity, unless its charter proclaims and effectively prescribes first, respect for the human person in all men, no matter what their social positions; second, acknowledgment of the solidarity of all people in forming the human family, created by the loving omnipotence of God; third, the imperative demand on society to place the common good above personal gain, the service of each for all. When the spirit of man is reformed and stabilized according to these truths, the condition of the workingman will be improved (International Labor, 712).

Popes Pius XI and Pius XII state that the foundation must be right order as planned by God.

Even though economics and moral science employ each its own principles in its own sphere, it is, nevertheless, an error to say that the economic and moral orders are so distinct from and alien to each other that the former depends in no way on the latter. Certainly the laws of economics, as they are termed, being based on the very nature of material things and on the capacities of the human body and mind, determine the limits of what productive human effort cannot and of what it can attain in the economic field and by what means. Yet it is reason itself that clearly shows, on the basis of the individual and social nature of things and of men, the purpose which God ordained for all economic life [QUADRAGESIMO ANNO, 42].

. . . If all these relations are properly maintained the various occupations will combine and coalesce into, as it were, a single body and like members of the body mutually aid and complete one another. For then only will the social economy be rightly established and attain its purposes when all and each are supplied with all the goods that the wealth and resources of nature, technical achievement, and the social organization of economic life can furnish. And these goods ought indeed to be enough both to meet the demands of necessity and decent comfort and to advance people to that happier and fuller condition of life which, when it is wisely cared for, is not only no hindrance to virtue but helps it greatly [QUADRAGESIMO ANNO, 75].

No genuine cure can be furnished for this lamentable ruin of souls, which, so long as it continues, will frustrate all efforts to regenerate society, unless men return openly and sincerely to the teaching of the Gospel, to the precepts of Him Who alone has the words of everlasting life (Cf. John 6:69), words which will never pass away, even if Heaven and earth will pass away (Cf. Matt. 24:35). All experts in social problems are seeking eagerly a structure so fashioned in accordance with the norms of reason that it can lead economic life back to sound and right order. But this order, which We Ourselves ardently long for and with all Our efforts promote, will be wholly defective and incomplete unless all the activities of men harmoniously unite to imitate and attain, in so far as it lies within human strength, the marvelous unity of the Divine plan. We mean that perfect order which the Church with great force and power preaches and which right human reason itself demands, that all things be directed to God as the first and supreme end of all created activity, and that all created good under God be considered as mere instruments to be used only in so far as they conduce to the attainment of the supreme end. Nor is it to be thought that gainful occupations are thereby belittled or judged less consonant with human dignity; on the contrary, we are taught to recognize in them with reverence the manifest will of the Divine Creator Who placed man upon the earth to work it and use it in a multitude of ways for his needs. Those who are engaged in producing goods, therefore, are not forbidden to increase their fortune in a just and lawful manner; for it is only fair that he who renders service to the community and makes it richer should also, through the increased wealth of the community, be made richer himself according to his position, provided that all these things be sought with due respect for the laws of God and without impairing the rights of others and that they be employed in accordance with faith and right reason. If these principles are observed by everyone, everywhere, and always, not only the production and acquisition of goods but also the use of wealth, which now is seen to be so often contrary to right order, will be brought back soon within the bounds of equity and just distribution. The sordid love of wealth, which is the shame and great sin of our age, will be opposed in actual fact by the gentle yet effective law of Christian moderation which commands man to seek first the Kingdom of God and His justice, with the assurance that, by virtue of God's kindness and unfailing promise, temporal goods also, in so far as he has need of them, shall be given him besides (Cf. Matt. 6:33) [QUADRAGESIMO ANNO, 136].

The strength of an organization, no matter how powerful one may consider it to be, is not of itself an element of order. Recent and current history gives continuously tragic proof. Whoever has eyes to see can easily convince himself of this. Today, as yesterday, in the future as in the past, a firm and solid position can be built only on the foundations laid by nature, and in reality by the Creator, as the basis of the sole genuine stability (Belgian Workers, 61).

Where God is not beginning and end, where the order that reigns in His Creation is not a guide and measure of the freedom and activity of everyone, unity among men cannot be achieved. The material conditions of life and labor, taken in themselves, and resting upon an alleged uniformity of interests, can never form the basis of the unity of the working class. Would not the attempt to build on such a foundation amount clearly to an act of violence against nature, and would it not serve merely to create new oppressions and divisions within the human family, at a moment when every honest laboring man yearns for just and peaceful organization in private and public economy and over the whole range of social life (Labor's Dignity, 304-305)?

Pope Pius XII deprecates the errors committed in ordering economic life by those who ignore the true nature of man and society and place all their confidence in legal arrangements.

. . . there is much talk nowadays about reforming the structure of industry. Those who promote it think primarily of legal modifications among its members, be they businessmen or employes included in the business by virtue of their labor contract.

We cannot lose sight of the tendencies infiltrating such movements. These tendencies do not, as is claimed, apply the incontestible norms of natural law to the changed conditions of the time, but simply exclude them. . . . We opposed these tendencies, not to favor the material interests of one group over another, but to assure sincerity and tranquility of conscience for all those to whom these problems apply (Italian Employers, 571).

Thus, these planners overlook the positive approach of building an economic system on the occupational or corporative order which rests on the principle of the organic unity of society.

. . . the words of great wisdom of Our glorious predecessor, Pius XI, were distorted. These distortions give today the weight and importance of a social policy of the Church to an observation of secondary importance regarding eventual legal adjustments in the relations between the workers as members of the labor contract and the other contracting party. Meanwhile they pass over more or less in silence the chief part of the encyclical QUADRAGESIMO ANNO, which contains that social policy embodying the idea of an occupational, corporative order of the whole economy (Italian Employers, 571).

Many who ignore this principle succumb to the error of collectivism.

Those who set about treating questions relating to the reform of the structure of industry without taking into account that every single business is by its own purpose closely tied to the whole of the national economy, run the risk of laying down erroneous and false premises with danger to the entire economic and social order. Therefore, in Our address of June 3, 1950, We tried to place in its proper light the thought and doctrine of Our predecessor, to whom nothing was more alien than any encouragement to follow the road which leads toward forms of anonymous, collective responsibility (Italian Employers, 571-572).

An economic order based on Christian brotherhood in the Fatherhood of God and on man, his personal dignity and worth and his social character, will lead to economic success in business and organic unity in society.

The great misery of the social order is that it is not deeply Christian nor really human, but only technical and economic. It is not built on what should be its basis and the solid foundation of its unity—the common character of men by their nature and their sonship of God through the grace of divine adoption.

As for you who are resolved to introduce everywhere this human factor into business, in the various grades and offices which comprise it and in economic and public life by legislation and popular education, you try to transform the masses . . . into a society whose members, while differing from one another, constitute, each according to his function, one united body.

.   .   .   .

You walk the one, safe road; that which tends to give a soul to personal relationships by a sense of Christian brotherhood; a road that is practicable everywhere and one which moves widely on the level of a business firm. Your aim will render you capable of seeing that the personal dignity of the workers, far from being lost in the general management of a business itself, will increase the efficiency of the business, not only materially, but also and primarily by gaining the values of a true community (Italian Employers, 571-572).

"For Christ alone is the 'corner stone' (Ephesians ii; 20) on which man and society can find stability and salvation" [SUMMI PONTIFICATUS, 95]. It is the Mystical Body, His Church—of which He is the Head—whom He has commissioned to lead man and society to the full realization of their being.

The Church living in the heart of man and man living in the bosom of the Church—here . . . is the most deeply rooted and efficacious union that can be conceived. Through this union the Church elevates man to the perfection of his being and of his vitality. In order to give to human society men formed thus: men established in their inviolable integrity as images of God, men proud of their personal dignity and of their healthy freedom, men justly jealous of their equality with their fellows in all that touches the most essential bases of man's dignity, men firmly attached to their land and traditions —men, in a word, characterized by this fourfold element; this is what gives to human society its solid foundation and obtains for it security, equilibrium, equality, normal development in space and time (Society, 199-200).

SOCIAL JUSTICE

Difficulties of Reorganization. As individuals, men are unable to reform the social system in which they find themselves. This difficulty is apprehended by Pope Pius XII when he considers the present mentality.

We may add that especially the complications of the economic and military order have made of society a huge machine, of which man is no longer master, of which, indeed, he is afraid. Continuity in time had always appeared essential to life in society, and it seemed that this could not be conceived if men were isolated from the past, present, and future. Now this is precisely the disturbing phenomenon of which we are today witnesses.

Too often of the past hardly anything is any longer known, or, at most, only what is sufficient to guess at its hazy outlines in the accumulation of its ruins.

The present is, for many, only the disordered rush of a torrent, which carries men like drift on its headlong course to the dark night of a future in which they will lose themselves with the stream that bears them on (Society, 202).

Duty to Reorganize. Reform can be affected by the organized effort of men acting together. This reorganization is a duty in social justice which falls upon *all*. First of all, the employers:

It happens all too frequently, however, under the salary system, that individual employers are helpless to ensure justice unless, with a view to its practice, they organize institutions the object of which is to prevent competition incompatible with fair treatment for the workers. Where this is true, it is the duty of contractors and employers to support and promote such necessary organizations as normal instruments enabling them to fulfill their obligations of justice [DIVINI REDEMPTORIS, 53].

Then, upon free organizations (such as unions) already existing:

And may these free organizations, now flourishing and rejoicing in their salutary fruits, set before themselves the task of preparing the way, in conformity with the mind of Christian social teaching, for those larger and more important guilds, Industries and Professions, which We mentioned before, and make every possible effort to bring them to realization [QUADRAGESIMO ANNO, 87].

Finally, upon all Christians:

A convinced Christian cannot confine himself within an easy and egotistical "isolationism," when he witnesses the needs and the misery of his brothers; when pleas for help come to him from these in economic distress; when he knows the aspiration of the working classes for more normal and just conditions of life; when he is aware of the abuses of an economic system which puts money above social obligations; when he is not ignorant of the aberrations of an intransigent nationalism which denies or spurns the common bonds linking the separate nations together and imposing on each one of them many and varied duties toward the great family of nations (Christmas 1948, 18).

In this process of reorganization the Church should be in the vanguard.

Now what is the consequence of all this for the Church? She must today, as never before, live her mission; she must reject more emphatically than ever that false and narrow concept of her spirituality and her interior life which would confine her, blind and mute, in the retirement of the sanctuary.

The Church cannot cut herself off, inert in the privacy of her churches, and thus desert her divinely providential mission of forming the complete man, and thereby collaborating without rest in the construction of the solid foundations of society. This mission is for her essential. Considered from this angle, the Church may be called the assembly of those who, under the supernatural influence of grace, in the perfection of their personal dignity as sons of God and in the harmonious development of all human inclinations and energies, build the powerful structure of human intercourse (Society, 200-201).

For as to these, the deposit of truth that God committed to Us and the grave duty of disseminating and interpreting the whole moral law, and of urging it in season and out of season, bring under and subject to Our supreme jurisdiction not only social order but economic activities themselves [QUADRAGESIMO ANNO, 41].

It is, on the other hand, the indisputable competence of the Church, on that side of the social order where it meets and enters into contact with the moral order, to decide whether the bases of a given social system are in accord with the unchangeable order which God, our Creator and Redeemer, has shown us through the natural law and Revelation, that twofold manifestation to which Leo XIII appeals in his Encyclical, and with reason: For the dictates of the natural law and the truths of Revelation spring forth in a different manner, like two streams of water that do not flow against one another but together from the same Divine Source; and the Church, guardian of the supernatural Christian order in which nature and grace converge, must form the consciences even of those who are called upon to find solutions for the problems and the duties imposed by social life. From the form given to society, whether conforming or not to the Divine law, depends and emerges the good or ill of souls, depends, that is, the decision whether men, all called to be revived by the grace of Christ, do actually in the detailed course of their life breathe the healthy vivifying atmosphere of truth and moral virtue or the disease-laden and often fatal air of error and corruption.

Before such a thought and such an anticipation how could the Church, loving mother that she is, solicitous for the welfare of her children, remain an indifferent onlooker in their danger, remain silent or feign not to see or take cognizance of social conditions which, whether one wills it or not, make difficult or practically impossible a Christian life in conformity with the precepts of the Divine Lawgiver (Pentecost, 3-4)?

MORAL REFORM

Guidance of the Church. The Popes repeatedly insist on religion and morality under the guidance of the Church as the necessary basis of all reform, with special reference to charity and justice.

And first and foremost, the entire body of religious teaching and practice, of which the Church is the interpreter and guardian, can pre-eminently bring together and unite the rich and the poor by recalling the two classes of society to their mutual duties, and in particular to those duties which derive from justice [RERUM NOVARUM, 29].

We approach the subject with confidence and surely by Our right, for the question under consideration is certainly one for which no satisfactory solution will be found unless religion and the Church have been called upon to aid. Moreover, since the safeguarding of religion and of all things within the jurisdiction of the Church is primarily Our stewardship, silence on Our part might be regarded as failure in Our duty. Assuredly, a question as formidable as this requires the attention and effort of others as well, namely, the heads of the State, employers and the rich, and, finally, those in whose behalf efforts are being made, the workers themselves. Yet without hesitation We affirm that if the Church is disregarded, human striving will be in vain. Manifestly, it is the Church which draws from the Gospel the teachings through which the struggle can be composed entirely or, after its bitterness is removed, can certainly become more tempered. It is the Church, again, that strives not only to instruct the mind but to regulate by her precepts the life and morals of individuals, that ameliorates the condition of the workers through her numerous and beneficent institutions, and that wishes and aims to have the thought and energy of all classes of society united to this end, that the interests of the workers be protected as fully as possible [RERUM NOVARUM, 24-25].

From the focal point of our Catholic life—the Mass— we find the strongest support of human society.

Every day, from where the sun rises to where it sets, without distinction of peoples or nations, there is offered a clean oblation, at which are present all children of the Church scattered throughout the world, and all find there a refuge in their needs and security in their perils (Society, 203).

Necessity of Moral Reform. The observance of the law of God, which Pope Pius XII calls society's "center of gravity" (Christmas 1942, 20-21), is fundamental to social order. The Sovereign Pontiffs constantly reiterate this truth. Pope Leo XIII reminds us of it a number of times.

For it is the opinion of some, which is caught up by the masses, that "the social question," as they call it, is merely "economic." The precise opposite is the truth, that it is first of all moral and religious, and for that reason its solution is to be expected mainly from the moral law and the pronouncements of religion [GRAVES DE COMMUNI, 174].

And since religion alone, as We said in the beginning, can remove the evil, root and branch, let all reflect upon this: First and foremost Christian morals must be re-established, without which even the weapons of prudence, which are considered especially effective, will be of no avail to secure well-being [RERUM NOVARUM, 82].

Pope Benedict XV affirms that we must bring "Christian principles into honor, if we have any real desire for the peace and harmony of human society" [AD BEATISSIMI, p. 204].

Pope Pius XI repeatedly insists that

No genuine cure can be furnished for this lamentable ruin of souls, which, so long as it continues, will frustrate all efforts to regenerate society, unless men return openly and sincerely to the teaching of the Gospel, to the precepts of Him Who alone has the words of everlasting life, words which will never pass away, even if Heaven and earth will pass away [QUAD-RAGESIMO ANNO, 136].

Yet, if we look into the matter more carefully and more thoroughly, we shall clearly perceive that, preceding this ardently desired social restoration, there must be a renewal of the Christian spirit, from which so many immersed in economic life have, far and wide, unhappily fallen away, lest all our efforts be wasted and our house be builded not on a rock but on shifting sand [QUADRAGESIMO ANNO, 127].

". . . two things are especially necessary: reform of institutions and correction of morals" [QUADRAGESIMO ANNO, 77].

"What We have taught about the reconstruction and perfection of social order can surely in no wise be brought to realization without reform of morality, the very record of history clearly shows" [QUADRAGESIMO ANNO, 97].

As in all the stormy periods of the history of the Church, the fundamental remedy today lies in a sincere renewal of private and public life according to the principles of the Gospel by all those who belong to the Fold of Christ, that they may be in truth the salt of the earth to preserve human society from total corruption [DIVINI REDEMPTORIS, 41].

Pope Pius XII concurs in these words:

No power of the State will reform the spirit of man. That is the sacred office of Religion. And the State whose foundations rest on Morality and Religion will be the surest protector and defender of the workingman (International Labor, 712).

Pope Pius XII applies the principle more specifically to labor.

The most effective leaven—we can say the only really effective one—to create this sense of solidarity, this sure guarantee of rectitude and social peace resides in the spirit of the Gospel and flows to you from the Heart of the God-Man, Saviour of the World. No laborer has ever been so perfectly, so profoundly penetrated by it as he who lived with Christ in the closest intimacy and communion of family and labor, His foster father, St. Joseph. Under his powerful patronage we place our Catholic labor associations, so that they, in the hour of such important decisions and dangers for all the labor of the world, may fully accomplish their providential mission (Italian Workers 1945, 22).

In the following passage he shows in what way the social question is a moral and religious question.

It [victory over the world by faith] *must be a victory over social miseries, that they may be overcome with the force of justice and love.*
The social question . . . is undoubtedly an economic question also, but even more than that it is a question which concerns the ordered regulation of human society. And, in its

deepest sense, it is a moral and, therefore, a religious question. As such it may be summed up thus: have men—from the individual to the people, and right through to the community of peoples—the moral strength to create such public conditions that in the life of society there will not be any individuals or any peoples who are merely objects, that is to say, deprived of all right and exposed to exploitation by others, but all instead will be subjects, that is, having a legitimate share in the formation of the social order, and able, according to their art or profession, to live happily and tranquilly with sufficient means of support, protected effectively against the violences of an egoistic economy, in freedom defined by the general welfare, and with full human dignity, each respecting his neighbor as he respects himself (Catholic Action, 53)?

Pope Pius XII also links the social question directly to its fundamental remedy.

Will humanity be capable of generating and possessing the moral strength to realize such a social order? In any case, one thing is certain: that strength can be drawn from one wellspring only, from the Catholic faith lived to its ultimate consequences and nourished by the supra-human streams of grace which the Divine Redeemer bestows on humanity with faith itself. One generation alone which believes like this can give the human family the peace it longs for (Catholic Action, 53-54).

Ignoring Necessity of Reform. He also warns of the consequences of ignoring this remedy.

The origin and the primary scope of social life is the conservation, development, and perfection of the human person, helping him to realize accurately the demands and values of religion and culture set by the Creator for every man and for all mankind, both as a whole and in its natural ramifications. A social teaching or a social reconstruction program which denies or prescinds from this internal essential relation to God of everything that regards man, is on a false course; and while it builds up with one hand, it prepares with the other the materials which sooner or later will undermine and destroy the whole fabric. And when it disregards the respect due to the human person and to the life which is proper to that person, and gives no thought to it in its organization, in legislative and executive activity, then instead of serving society, it harms it . . . (Christmas 1942, 5).

Again:

Before all else, it is certain that the radical and ultimate cause of the evils which We deplore in modern society is the denial and rejection of a universal norm of morality as well for individual and social life as for international relations; We mean the disregard, so common nowadays, and the forgetfulness of the natural law itself, which has its foundation in God, Almighty Creator and Father of all, supreme and absolute Lawgiver, all-wise and just Judge of human actions. When God is hated, every basis of morality is undermined; the voice of conscience is stilled or at any rate grows very faint, that voice which teaches even to the illiterate and to uncivilized tribes what is good and what is bad, what lawful, what forbidden, and makes men feel themselves responsible for their actions to a Supreme Judge [SUMMI PONTIFICATUS, 23].

Application to Social Organization. Making a practical application of the above truths to social organization, Pope Leo explains:

Wherefore, if human society is to be healed, only a return to Christian life and institutions will heal it. In the case of decaying societies it is most correctly prescribed that, if they wish to be regenerated, they must be recalled to their origins. For the perfection of all associations is this, namely, to work for and to attain the purpose for which they were formed, so that all social actions should be inspired by the same principle which brought the society itself into being. Wherefore, turning away from the original purpose is corruption, while going back to this purpose is recovery, and just as we affirm this as unquestionably true of the entire body of the commonwealth in like manner we affirm it of that order of citizens who sustain life by labor and who constitute the vast majority of society [RERUM NOVARUM, 41].

It is clear, however, that moral and religious perfection ought to be regarded as their principal goal, and that their social organization as such ought above all to be directed completely by this goal. For otherwise they would degenerate in nature and would be little better than those associations in which no account is ordinarily taken of religion [RERUM NOVARUM, 77].

Pope Pius XII re-emphasizes the principle.

From this expectation arise problems of reconstruction for the laboring classes, plans for structural reform, and ideas concerning property and enterprise which at times are conceived passionately, precipitately, and confusedly as regards doctrinal content. But they will have to be faced with the inescapable norms of reason and of Faith, which, according to its duty, the teaching of the Church must define (Semaines 1945, 618).

Justice and Charity. Justice and charity are basic to this moral and religious reform.

. . . the re-education of mankind must be, above all things, spiritual and religious. Hence, it must proceed from Christ as from its indispensable foundation; must be actuated by justice and crowned by charity [SUMMI PONTIFICATUS, 76].

Because of its nature, justice is essential to the social order. Pope Pius XII explains the imperative necessity of this virtue flowing from its nature as well as the nature of man and society.

. . . the most specific object of juridical science is . . . justice, in its high function of regulating the balance of individual and social needs in the bosom of the human family.

Justice is not merely an abstract concept, an external ideal to which institutions must seek to conform as far as possible in a given historical moment. It is above all something inherent in man, in society, in its fundamental institutions, because of that sum total of practical principles which it dictates and imposes, of those more universal norms of conduct which form part of the objective human and civil order established by the perfect mind of the First Maker (Jurists, 56).

Obligations of Social Justice. What does social justice demand? The Popes specify obligations following from justice.

In reality, besides commutative justice, there is also social justice with its own set obligations, from which neither employers nor workingmen can escape. Now it is of the very essence of social justice to demand from each individual all that is necessary for the common good. But just as in the living organism it is impossible to provide for the good of the whole unless each single part and each individual member is given what it needs for the exercise of its proper functions, so it is impossible to care for the social organism and the good of society as a unit unless each single part and each individual member—that is to say, each individual man in the dignity of his human personality—is supplied with all that is necessary for the exercise of his social function. If social justice be satisfied, the result will be an intense activity in economic life as a whole, pursued in tranquillity and order. This activity will be proof of the health of the social body, just as the health of the human body is recognized in the undisturbed regularity and perfect efficiency of the whole organism [DIVINI REDEMPTORIS, 51].

To each, therefore, must be given his own share of goods, and the distribution of created goods, which, as every discerning person knows, is laboring today under the gravest evils due to the huge disparity between the few exceedingly rich and the unnumbered propertyless, must be effectively called back to and brought into conformity with the norms of the common good, that is, social justice [QUADRAGESIMO ANNO, 58].

That justice called commutative commands sacred respect for the division of possessions and forbids invasion of others' rights through the exceeding of the limits of one's own property; but the duty of owners to use their property only in a right way does not come under this type of justice, but under other virtues, obligations of which "cannot be enforced by legal action" [QUADRAGESIMO ANNO, 47].

Justice imposes obligations on both the employer and laborer.

It happens all too frequently, however, under the salary system, that individual employers are helpless to ensure justice unless, with a view to its practice, they organize institutions the object of which is to prevent competition incompatible with fair treatment for the workers. Where this is true, it is the duty of contractors and employers to support and promote such necessary organizations as normal instruments enabling them to fulfil their obligations of justice. But the laborers too must be mindful of their duty to love and deal fairly with their employers, and persuade themselves that there is no better means of safeguarding their own interests [DIVINI REDEMPTORIS, 53].

But it does violate right order when capital hires workers, that is, the non-owning working class, with a view to and under such terms that it directs business and even the whole economic system according to its own will and advantage, scorning the human dignity of the workers, the social character of economic activity and social justice itself, and the common good [QUADRAGESIMO ANNO, 101].

Hence it is contrary to social justice when, for the sake of personal gain and without regard for the common good, wages and salaries are excessively lowered or raised; and this same social justice demands that wages and salaries be so managed, through agreement of plans and wills, in so far as can be done, as to offer to the greatest possible number the opportunity of getting work and obtaining suitable means of livelihood [QUAD-RAGESIMO ANNO, 74].

Now if the rich and the prosperous are obliged out of ordinary motives of pity to act generously towards the poor their obligation is all the greater to do them justice. The salaries of the workers, as is just, are to be such that they are sufficient to maintain them and their families [SERTUM LAETI-TIAE, 36].

A right proportion among wages and salaries also contributes directly to the same results; and with this is closely connected a right proportion in the prices at which the goods are sold that are produced by the various occupations, such as agriculture, manufacturing, and others. If all these relations are properly maintained, the various occupations will combine and coalesce into, as it were, a single body and like members of the body mutually aid and complete one another. For then only will the social economy be rightly established and attain its purposes when all and each are supplied with all the goods that the wealth and resources of nature, technical achievement, and the social organization of economic life can furnish. And these goods ought indeed to be enough both to meet the demands of necessity and decent comfort and to advance people to that happier and fuller condition of life which, when it is wisely cared for, is not only no hindrance to virtue but helps it greatly [QUADRAGESIMO ANNO, 75].

If a just wage is not possible under the existing situation, reforms must be brought about.

It is obvious that, as in the case of ownership, so in the case of work, especially work hired out to others, there is a social aspect also to be considered in addition to the personal or individual aspect. For man's productive effort cannot yield its fruits unless a truly social and organic body exists, unless a social and juridical order watches over the exercise of work, unless the various occupations, being interdependent, cooperate with and mutually complete one another, and, what is still more important, unless mind, material things, and work combine and form as it were a single whole. Therefore, where the social and individual nature of work is neglected, it will be impossible to evaluate work justly and pay it according to justice [QUADRAGESIMO ANNO, 69].

In determining the amount of the wage, the condition of a business and of the one carrying it on must also be taken into account; for it would be unjust to demand excessive wages which a business cannot stand without its ruin and consequent calamity to the workers. If, however, a business makes too little money, because of lack of energy or lack of initiative or because of indifference to technical and economic progress, that must not be regarded a just reason for reducing the compensation of the workers. But if the business in question is not making enough money to pay the workers an equitable wage because it is being crushed by unjust burdens or forced to sell its product at less than a just price, those who are thus the cause of the injury are guilty of grave wrong, for they deprive workers of their just wage and force them under the pinch of necessity to accept a wage less than fair [QUADRAGESIMO ANNO, 72].

Justice alone is not sufficient. To it must be linked charity.

First, so as to avoid the reefs of individualism and collectivism, the twofold character, that is individual and social, both of capital or ownership and of work or labor must be given due and rightful weight. Relations of one to the other must be made to conform to the laws of strictest justice—commutative justice, as it is called—with the support, however, of Christian charity [QUADRAGESIMO ANNO, 110].

Meaning of Charity. Charity, establishing a union of hearts and minds, will supply the principle of stability needed to bring about social solidarity. What is this true Christian charity? Pope Pius XI tells us in the following passages:

But in effecting all this, the law of charity, "which is the bond of perfection," (Col. 3:14) must always take a leading role. How completely deceived, therefore, are those rash reformers who concern themselves with the enforcement of justice alone—and this, commutative justice—and in their pride reject the assistance of charity! Admittedly, no vicarious charity can substitute for justice which is due as an obligation and is wrongfully denied. Yet even supposing that everyone should finally receive all that is due him, the widest field for charity will always remain open. For justice alone can, if faithfully observed, remove the causes of social conflict but can never bring about union of minds and hearts. Indeed all the institutions for the establishment of peace and the promotion of mutual help among men, however perfect these may seem, have the principal foundation of their stability in the mutual bond of minds and hearts whereby the members are united with one another. If this bond is lacking, the best of regulations come to naught, as we have learned by too frequent experience. And so, then only will true co-operation be possible for a single common good when the constituent parts of society deeply feel themselves members of one great family and children of the same Heavenly Father; nay, that they are one body in Christ, "but severally members one of another" (Rom. 12:5) so that "if one member suffers anything, all the members suffer with it" (I Cor. 12:26). For then the rich and others in positions of power will change their former indifference toward their poorer brothers into a solicitous and active love, listen with kindliness to their just demands, and freely forgive their possible mistakes and faults. And the workers, sincerely putting aside every feeling of hatred or envy which the promoters of social conflict so cunningly exploit, will not only accept without rancor the place in human society assigned them by Divine Providence, but rather will hold it in esteem, knowing well that everyone according to his function and duty is toiling usefully and honorably for the common good and is following closely in the footsteps of Him Who, being in the form of God, willed to be a carpenter among men and be known as the son of a carpenter [QUADRAGESIMO ANNO, 137].

Still more important as a remedy for the evil we are considering, or certainly more directly calculated to cure it, is the precept of charity. We have in mind that Christian charity, "patient and kind," which avoids all semblance of demeaning paternalism, and all ostentation; that charity which from the very beginning of Christianity won to Christ the poorest of the poor, the slaves. And We are grateful to all those members of charitable associations, from the conferences of St. Vincent de

Paul to the recent great relief organizations, which are perseveringly practicing the spiritual and corporal works of mercy. The more the workingmen and the poor realize what the spirit of love animated by the virtue of Christ is doing for them, the more readily will they abandon the false persuasion that Christianity has lost its efficacy and that the Church stands on the side of the exploiters of their labor.

But when on the one hand We see thousands of the needy, victims of real misery for various reasons beyond their control, and on the other so many round about them who spend huge sums of money on useless things and frivolous amusement, We cannot fail to remark with sorrow not only that justice is poorly observed, but that the precept of charity also is not sufficiently appreciated, is not a vital thing in daily life [DIVINI REDEMPTORIS, 46-47].

Inclusion of All. Whom does it include?

The Christian law of charity . . . is large enough to embrace all ranks as belonging to one and the same family, the offspring of the same all-beneficent Father, redeemed by one Saviour, and called to the same eternal inheritance. This is, indeed, the Apostle's doctrine and monition: *One body and one Spirit, as you are called in one hope of your calling; one Lord, one faith, one baptism; one God and Father of all, who is above all, and through all, and in us all* (Eph. 4:4-6). Wherefore, because of the natural co-ordination of the working classes with the other ranks of society, which is made more intimate by the law of Christian brotherhood, it surely follows that whatever diligence is bestowed upon assisting the working classes must extend to these other classes—the more because it is clearly proper and even necessary, if the work is to be successful . . . [GRAVES DE COMMUNI, pp. 172-173].

By the law of mutual charity, which, as it were, completes the law of justice, we are bidden not only to give to all their due and interfere with the rights of none, but also to do kindnesses one to another *not in word nor in tongue, but in deed and in truth* (I John 3:18), remembering what Christ most lovingly said to His disciples: *A new commandment I give unto you, that you love one another, as I have loved you, that you also love one another. By this shall all men know that you are My disciples, if you have love one for another* (John 13:34, 35). Such zeal for doing kindnesses, though it ought to be first of all solicitous about the eternal good of souls, should yet by no means neglect what is good and useful for this life. Here it is worthy of remark that Christ, when the disciples of the Baptist asked Him: "Art thou He that art to come, or look we for another?" grounded the evidence for the office intrusted to Him among mankind on this particular work of charity, recalling the phrase of Isaiah: *The blind see, the lame walk, the lepers are cleansed, the deaf hear, the dead rise again, the poor have the Gospel preached to them* (Matt. 11:5). Speaking also of the last judgment and the rewards and punishments to be then adjudged, He declared that He would particularly examine the charity men had used one towards another. In this discourse of Christ it is indeed wonderful how, leaving unmentioned that side of compassion that ministers to the soul, He spoke only of the offices of bodily compassion, and of them as being bestowed upon Himself: *I was hungry, and you gave Me to eat; I was thirsty, and you gave Me to drink; I was a stranger, and you took Me in; sick, and you visited Me; I was in prison, and you came to Me* (Matt. 25:35, 36) [GRAVES DE COMMUNI, p. 175].

What is its effect?

To be sure of eternal life, therefore, and to be able to help the poor effectively, it is imperative to return to a more moderate way of life, to renounce the joys, often sinful, which the world today holds out in such abundance; to forget self for love of the neighbor. There is a divine regenerating force in this "new precept" (as Christ called it) of Christian charity (John 13:34) [DIVINI REDEMPTORIS, 48].

Pope Pius XI promises that, "its faithful observance will pour into the heart an inner peace which the world knows not, and will finally cure the ills which oppress humanity" [DIVINI REDEMPTORIS, 48]. In fact, charity is a primary necessity to an effective solution, as Pope Pius X notes in his letter to the French Archbishops and Bishops when condemning Le Sillon.

For if one wishes to reach—and we desire to do so with all our heart—the highest possible summit of well-being for society and for each of its members by means of fraternity or, as it is called, by universal solidarity, there is needed the union of minds in the truth, the union of wills in morality, the union of hearts in the love of God and of His Son Jesus Christ. But this union is only attainable by Catholic charity, which alone, consequently, can lead the people in the march of progress towards the ideal of civilization (Sillon, 702).

Partnership of Justice and Charity. Justice and charity must complement each other.

. . . the institutions themselves of peoples, and particularly those of all social life, ought to be penetrated with this justice, and it is most necessary that it be truly effective, that is, establish a juridical and social order which will, as it were, give form and shape to all economic life. Social charity, moreover, ought to be as the soul of this order, an order which public authority ought to be ever ready effectively to protect and defend [QUADRAGESIMO ANNO, 88].

But charity will never be true charity unless it takes justice into constant account. The Apostle teaches that "he that loveth his neighbor hath fulfilled the law" and he gives the reason: "For, *Thou shalt not commit adultery, Thou shalt not kill, Thou shalt not steal* . . . and if there be any other commandment, it is comprised in this word: *Thou shalt love thy neighbor as thyself*" (Rom. 13:8, 9). According to the Apostle, then, all the commandments, including those which are of strict justice, as those which forbid us to kill or to steal, may be reduced to the single precept of true charity. From this it follows that a "charity" which deprives the workingman of the salary to which he has a strict title in justice, is not charity at all, but only its empty name and hollow semblance. The wage earner is not to receive as alms what is his due in justice. And let no one attempt with trifling charitable donations to exempt himself from the great duties imposed by justice. Both justice and charity often dictate obligations touching on the same subject matter, but under different aspects; and the very dignity of the workingman makes him justly and acutely sensitive to the duties of others in his regard [DIVINI REDEMPTORIS, 49].

Pope Pius XII likewise points out that charity cannot be a substitute for justice, but "must always take into account the justice which must be established and must never satisfy itself with palliating disorders and the deficiencies of some unjust situation" (Semaines 1952, 12). He demonstrates the necessity of this partnership between justice and charity:

If Charity be not joined with strict and rigid justice, in a kind of brotherly bond, the eye of the mind is very easily clouded and thereby hindered, so that it does not discern the rights of another; the ears become deaf, so that they do not hear the voice of that Equity which has the power, by explanation to the wise man willing to listen, to make clear in reasonable and orderly fashion whatever may be matter of dispute, even the bitterest and the rudest of differences (Easter, 131).

Indeed, in not a few countries, falsehood instead of truth has been presented under a certain guise of reasonableness; not love, not charity, have been fostered, but hatred and a blind rivalry are being encouraged; not concord among citizens is exalted, but disturbance and disorder are being provoked.

However, as sincere and thoughtful persons recognize, it is not in this way that either the problems which still separate nations can be solved, or the proletariat classes be guided, as they should, towards a better future. Never, be it said, has hatred or lying or disorder generated any good. Unquestionably, people who are needy should be raised to a status that is worthy of man; yet, not with force, not with violence, but with laws that are just. What must certainly be done, under the auspices of truth and the guidance of justice, is to eliminate as soon as possible all the differences which separate and divide peoples [SUMMI MAERORIS, 628].

This partnership of justice and charity as a guiding principle must replace unrestricted competition as well as economic dictatorship flowing from rugged individualism.

Just as the unity of human society cannot be founded on an opposition of classes, so also the right ordering of economic life cannot be left to a free competition of forces. For from this source, as from a poisoned spring, have originated and spread all the errors of individualist economic teaching. Destroying through forgetfulness or ignorance the social and moral character of economic life, it held that economic life must be considered and treated as altogether free from and independent of public authority, because in the market, i.e., in the free struggle of competitors, it would have a principle of self-direction which governs it much more perfectly than would the intervention of any created intellect. But free competition, while justified and certainly useful provided it is kept within certain limits, clearly cannot direct economic life—a truth which the outcome of the application in practice of the tenets of this evil individualistic spirit has more than sufficiently demonstrated. Therefore, it is most necessary that economic life be again subjected to and governed by a true and effective directing principle. This function is one that the economic dictatorship which has recently displaced free competition can still less perform, since it is a headstrong power and a violent energy that, to benefit people, needs to be strongly curbed and wisely ruled. But it cannot curb and rule itself. Loftier and nobler principles—social justice and social charity—must, therefore, be sought whereby this dictatorship may be governed firmly and fully [QUADRAGESIMO ANNO, 88].

The reign of justice and charity is possible only under economic organization.

If, therefore, We consider the whole structure of economic life, as We have already pointed out in Our Encyclical QUAD-RAGESIMO ANNO, the reign of mutual collaboration between justice and charity in social-economic relations can only be achieved by a body of professional and interprofessional organizations, built on solidly Christian foundations, working together to effect, under forms adapted to different places and circumstances, what has been called the Corporation [DIVINI REDEMPTORIS, 54].

The functional roles in this partnership of justice and charity are specified by Pope Pius XII when he says: "And let men set about their peaceful work of abundant production for the common welfare—with justice their guide and charity their motive" [AUSPICIA QUAEDAM, p. 418].

Chapter XIII

Use of Material Goods; Private Property

USE OF MATERIAL GOODS

Equitable Distribution. In referring to the use of material goods, the Popes emphasize equitable distribution, the correct attitude toward material things and the stewardship of owners. "The fundamental point of the social question is this, that the goods created by God for all men should in the same way reach all, justice guiding and charity helping" [SERTUM LAETITIAE, 34].

Those who are engaged in producing goods, therefore, are not forbidden to increase their fortune in a just and lawful manner; for it is only fair that he who renders service to the community and makes it richer should also, through the increased wealth of the community, be made richer himself according to his position, provided that all these things be sought with due respect for the laws of God and without impairing the rights of others and that they be employed in accordance with faith and right reason. If these principles are observed by everyone, everywhere, and always, not only the production and acquisition of goods but also the use of wealth,

154

which now is seen to be so often contrary to right order, will be brought back soon within the bounds of equity and just distribution [QUADRAGESIMO ANNO, 136].

. . . seeing that all are "eating at the same table," so to speak, it would seem just that—while respecting differences in functions and responsibilities—the share given to each should conform to a common dignity which they have as men, and that in particular these shares should permit a greater number of persons to attain the independence and security which come from possession of private property, and to participate with their families in the spiritual and cultural goods to which earthly goods are ordered (Semaines 1952, 12).

Distribution may not be surrendered to the "free play of blind economic forces" but must be considered in the perspective of the common good.

To meet the demands of the social life, such a distribution cannot be left to the free play of blind economic forces, but must be faced on the level of the national economy, because it is from there that one gets a clear view of the end to be pursued in the service of the common temporal good (Semaines 1952).

However, in securing equitable distribution Pope Pius XII warns against another extreme. He says that ". . . the various forms and methods of such institutions [to correct evils of maldistribution] should be studied with great care, and one could not possibly commit oneself unreservedly to a plan wherein policies of excessive taxation might endanger the rights of private property and where abuses of collective security could weaken the rights of the person and the family" (Semaines 1952, 12).

Thus the Church holds "a position midway between the errors of liberalism and statism . . ." (Semaines 1952, 12).

Justice requires . . . that the infinite wealth and resources with which God has endowed the whole of the earth, shall be distributed, in conformity with right reason, for the use of all His children (Easter, 130-131).

Therefore, there are limitations regarding superfluous wealth.

Furthermore, a person's superfluous income, that is, income which he does not need to sustain life fittingly and with dignity, is not left wholly to his own free determination. Rather the Sacred Scriptures and the Fathers of the Church constantly declare in most explicit language that the rich are bound by a very grave precept to practice almsgiving, beneficence, and munificence [QUADRAGESIMO ANNO, 50].

As is very apparent, this just distribution does not obtain today in our economy. Pope Pius makes this observation:

To each, therefore, must be given his own share of goods, and the distribution of created goods, which, as every discerning person knows, is laboring today under the gravest evils due to the huge disparity between the few exceedingly rich and the unnumbered propertyless, must be effectively called back to and brought into conformity with the norms of the common good, that is, social justice [QUADRAGESIMO ANNO, 58].

Consequently, an unwarranted and unjust exercise of power is wielded by those who control wealth in the form of credit.

This dictatorship is being most forcibly exercised by those who, since they hold the money and completely control credit, also rule the lending of money. Hence they regulate the flow, so to speak, of the life-blood whereby the entire economic system lives, and have so firmly in their grasp the soul, as it were, of economic life that no one can breathe against their will [QUADRAGESIMO ANNO, 106].

Correct Attitude Toward Material Goods. An explanation of the real purpose of material goods and their place in God's design is given to us in the words of Pope Leo XIII and Pope Pius XI.

We cannot understand and evaluate mortal things rightly unless the mind reflects upon the other life, the life which is immortal. If this other life indeed were taken away, the form and true notion of the right would immediately perish; nay, this entire world would become an enigma insoluble to man. Therefore, what we learn from nature itself as our teacher is also a Christian dogma and on it the whole system and structure of religion rests, as it were, on its main foundation; namely, that, when we have left this life, only then shall we truly begin to live. God has not created man for the fragile and transitory things of this world, but for Heaven and eternity, and He has ordained the earth as a place of exile, not as our permanent home. Whether you abound in, or whether you lack, riches, and all the other things which are called good, is of no importance in relation to eternal happiness. But how you use them, that is truly of utmost importance [RERUM NOVARUM, 33].

But the poor, too, in their turn, while engaged, according to the laws of charity and justice, in acquiring the necessities of life and also in bettering their condition, should always remain "poor in spirit," and hold spiritual goods in higher

esteem than earthly property and pleasures [DIVINI REDEMP-
TORIS, 45].

But it is of the very nature of material things that when
sought unrestrainedly they bring with them every sort of evil,
moral abasement and dissensions first of all. For as in themselves they are mean and common, they cannot satisfy the
noble aspirations of the human heart, which was created by
God and for God, and cannot rest until it finds the true rest
in God Himself.

And, further, as they are confined within narrow limits
the more they are shared the less there is for each, while on
the other hand the things of the spirit, the more widely they
are partaken of, enrich all without themselves ever diminishing.
Whence it comes that the things of the earth, inasmuch as
they cannot satisfy all alike or fill the desires of anyone, become causes of discord and sickness of spirit, as Solomon in
his wisdom said: *Vanity of vanities . . . and affliction of spirit.*
And this comes on society as on individuals. *From whence
are wars and contentions among you?* asked the Apostle James.
Are they not hence, from your concupiscences?

For no worse plague can be imagined, bringing trouble not
only to families but to States, than the "lust of the flesh," that
is the desire for pleasure; from the "lust of the eyes," that is
desire for gain, arise class warfare and social egoism; through
"pride of life," the desire of dominating others, comes party
strife, leading even to rebellion against authority, treason,
parricide of country [UBI ARCANO DEI, p. 302].

The picture of those who forget this teaching regarding
material goods is not a happy one. "Those who looked for
the salvation of society from the machinery of the world
economic market have remained thus disillusioned because
they had become not the lords and masters but the slaves

of material wealth, which they served without reference to the higher end of man, making it an end in itself" (Christmas 1943, 67-68).

But men of carnal mind, who love nothing but themselves, allow their thoughts to grovel upon things of earth until they are unable to lift them to that which is higher. For, far from using the goods of time as a help towards securing those which are eternal, they lose sight altogether of the world which is to come, and sink to the lowest depths of degradation. We may doubt if God could inflict upon a man a more terrible punishment than to allow him to waste his whole life in the pursuit of earthly pleasures, and in forgetfulness of the happiness which alone lasts forever [LAETITIAE SANCTAE, 5].

Pope Leo describes the resulting condition which would obtain in economic society if men would understand the real role of material goods assigned by God Himself in the correct ordering of society.

. . . the favor of God Himself seems to incline more toward the unfortunate as a class; for Jesus Christ calls the poor (Matt. 5:3) blessed, and He invites most lovingly all who are in labor or sorrow (Matt. 11:28) to come to Him for solace, embracing with special love the lowly and those harassed by injustice. At the realization of these things the proud spirit of the rich is easily brought down, and the downcast heart of the afflicted is lifted up; the former are moved toward kindness, the latter, toward reasonableness in their demands. Thus the distance between the classes which pride seeks is reduced, and it will easily be brought to pass that the two classes, with hands clasped in friendship, will be united in heart [RERUM NOVARUM, 37].

Man would approximate a more proper attitude and balance toward material goods if he maintained union with God in prayer and thus viewed all creation in His perspective.

In addition, prayer will remove the fundamental cause of present-day difficulties which We have mentioned above, that is the insatiable greed for earthly goods. The man who prays looks above to the goods of Heaven whereon he meditates and which he desires; his whole being is plunged in the contemplation of the marvelous order established by God, which knows not the frenzy of success and does not lose itself in futile competitions of ever increasing speed; and thus automatically, as it were, will be re-established that equilibrium between work and rest, whose entire absence from society today is responsible for grave dangers to life physical, economic, and moral. If therefore those who through the excessive production of manufactured articles have fallen into unemployment and poverty made up their minds to give the proper time to prayer there is no doubt that work and production would soon return to reasonable limits and that the conflict which now divides humanity into two great camps struggling for transient interests would be changed into a noble and peaceful contest for goods heavenly and eternal [CARITATE CHRISTI COMPULSI, 14-15].

And all should look to Christ for His example and encouragement.

But that poverty of the Lord and Creator of the world, deliberately willed by Him, a poverty which will accompany Him in the workshop of Nazareth and throughout His public life, signifies and portrays the command and the dominance He had over material things; and thus it shows with striking efficacy the natural and essential subjection of material goods to the life of the spirit and to higher cultural, moral, and religious perfection which is necessary for man endowed with reason (Christmas 1943, 67).

And Jesus Christ has confirmed this by fact and by deed, Who for the salvation of men, "being rich, became poor" (II Cor. 8:9); and although He was the Son of God and God Himself, yet He willed to seem and to be thought the son of a carpenter; nay, He even did not disdain to spend a great part of His life at the work of a carpenter. "Is not this the carpenter, the Son of Mary?" (Mark 6:3). Those who contemplate this Divine example will more easily understand these truths: True dignity and excellence in men resides in moral living, that is, in virtue; virtue is the common inheritance of man, attainable equally by the humblest and the mightiest, by the rich and the poor; and the reward of eternal happiness will follow upon virtue and merit alone, regardless of the person in whom they may be found [RERUM NOVARUM, 37].

. . . let them [Catholic deserters to Socialism] be convinced that nowhere, even on earth, can they find full happiness save with Him who, being rich, became poor for our sakes that through His poverty we might become rich (II Cor. 8:9), Who was poor and in labors from His youth, Who invited to Himself all that labor and are heavily burdened that He might refresh them fully in the love of His heart (Matt. 11:28), and Who, lastly, without any respect for persons will require more of them to whom more has been given (Cf. Luke 12:48) and "will render to everyone according to his conduct" (Matt. 16:27) [QUADRAGESIMO ANNO, 126].

It is Christianity that adores the Son of God, made Man for love of man, and become not only the "Son of a Carpenter" but Himself a "Carpenter" (Cf. Matt. 13:55; Mark 6:3). It was Christianity that raised manual labor to its true dignity, whereas it had hitherto been so despised that even the moderate Cicero did not hesitate to sum up the general opinion of his time in words of which any modern sociologist would be ashamed: "All artisans are engaged in sordid trades, for there can be nothing ennobling about a workshop" (Cicero, *De officiis,* Bk. I, c. 42) [DIVINI REDEMPTORIS, 36].

Stewardship of Wealth. Having shown that the goods of this world are not to be sought as an end in themselves, the Sovereign Pontiffs explain that our "ownership" of them consists only in a stewardship to be exercised in furthering God's designs and for which we must render an account.

And here We wish . . . to insist more particularly on two teachings of Our Lord which have a special bearing on the present condition of the human race: detachment from earthly goods and the precept of charity. "Blessed are the poor in spirit" (Matt. 5:3) were the first words that fell from the lips of the Divine Master in His sermon on the mount. This lesson is more than ever necessary in these days of materialism athirst for the goods and pleasures of this earth. All Christians, rich or poor, must keep their eye fixed on heaven, remembering that "we have not here a lasting city, but we seek one that is to come" (Hebrews 13:14). The rich should not place their happiness in things of earth nor spend their best efforts in the acquisition of them. Rather, considering themselves only as stewards of their earthly goods, let them be mindful of the account they must render of them to their Lord and Master, and value them as precious means that God has put into their hands for doing good; let them not fail, besides, to distribute of their abundance to the poor, according to the evangelical precept (Luke 11:41). Otherwise there shall be verified of them and their riches the harsh condemnation of St. James the Apostle: "Go to now, ye rich men; weep and howl in your miseries which shall come upon you. Your riches are corrupted, and your garments are moth-eaten; your gold and silver is cankered; and the rust of them shall be for a testimony against you and shall eat your flesh like fire. You have stored up to yourselves wrath against the last day . . ." (James 5:1-3) [DIVINI REDEMPTORIS, 44].

The foundation of this teaching [on the use of wealth] rests on this, that the just ownership of money is distinct from the just use of money [RERUM NOVARUM, 35].

Only thus can we and must we insure that private property and the use of material goods bring to society peace and prosperity and long life, that they no longer set up precarious conditions which will give rise to struggles and jealousies and which are left to the mercy and the blind interplay of force and weakness.

The native right to the use of material good, intimately linked as it is to the dignity and other rights of the human person together with the statutes [regulating the right to the use of the material goods of the earth] mentioned above, provides man with a secure material basis of the highest import on which to rise to the fulfillment with reasonable liberty of his moral duties.

The safe guardianship of this right will insure the personal dignity of man and will facilitate for him the attention to and fulfillment of that sum of stable duties and decisions for which he is directly responsible to his Creator. Man has, in truth, the entirely personal duty to preserve and order to perfection his material and spiritual life, so as to secure the religious and moral scope which God has assigned to all men and has given them as the supreme norm, obliging always and everywhere, before all other duties (Pentecost, 8-9).

Violation of Duties of Stewardship. Pope Pius XI describes the downward spiral into an abyss of gravest injustices, as seen in our present economy, when we lose sight of the proper use of material goods.

The ultimate consequences of the individualist spirit in economic life are those which you yourselves . . . see and deplore: Free competition has destroyed itself; economic dictatorship has supplanted the free market; unbridled ambition for power has likewise succeeded greed for gain; all economic life has become tragically hard, inexorable, and cruel. To these are to be added the grave evils that have resulted from an intermingling and shameful confusion of the functions and duties of public authority with those of the economic sphere—such as, one of the worst, the virtual degradation of the majesty of the State, which although it ought to sit on high like a queen and supreme arbitress, free from all partiality and intent upon the one common good and justice, is become a slave, surrendered and delivered to the passions and greed of men. And as to international relations, two different streams have issued from the one fountainhead: On the one hand, economic nationalism or even economic imperialism; on the other, a no less deadly and accursed internationalism of finance or international imperialism whose country is where profit is [QUADRAGESIMO ANNO, 109].

Thus it came to pass that many, much more than ever before, were solely concerned with increasing their wealth by any means whatsoever, and that in seeking their own selfish interests before everything else they had no conscience about committing even the gravest of crimes against others. Those first entering upon this broad way that leads to destruction easily found numerous imitators of their iniquity by the example of their manifest success, by their insolent display of wealth, by their ridiculing the conscience of others, who, as they said, were troubled by silly scruples, or lastly by crushing more conscientious competitors.

With the rulers of economic life abandoning the right road,

it was easy for the rank and file of workers everywhere to rush headlong also into the same chasm; and all the more so, because very many managements treated their workers like mere tools, with no concern at all for their souls, without indeed even the least thought of spiritual things. Truly the mind shudders at the thought of the grave dangers to which the morals of workers (particularly younger workers) and the modesty of girls and women are exposed in modern factories; when we recall how often the present economic scheme, and particularly the shameful housing conditions, create obstacles to the family bond and normal family life; when we remember how many obstacles are put in the way of the proper observance of Sundays and Holy Days; and when we reflect upon the universal weakening of that truly Christian sense through which even rude and unlettered men were wont to value higher things, and upon its substitution by the single preoccupation of getting in any way whatsoever one's daily bread. And thus bodily labor, which Divine Providence decreed to be performed, even after original sin, for the good at once of man's body and soul, is being everywhere changed into an instrument of perversion; for dead matter comes forth from the factory ennobled, while men there are corrupted and degraded [QUADRAGESIMO ANNO, 134, 135].

PRIVATE PROPERTY

A Natural Right. In assessing such aspects of the Industry Council Plan as the workers' sharing in the ownership, or the management, or the profits, it is necessary to keep in mind the Church's teaching on private property. First of all, it is a natural right and the foundation of every legitimate economic and social order.

Our immortal predecessor Leo XIII in his famous Encyclical RERUM NOVARUM already established the principle, that for every legitimate economic and social order "there must be laid down as the basic foundation the right of private property."

If it be true that the Church has always recognized "the natural right to property and of the hereditary transmission of one's own goods" (Encyclical QUADRAGESIMO ANNO), it is not less certain that this private property is in a special manner the natural fruit of labor, the product of an intense activity on the part of the man who acquires it through his energetic will to ensure and improve, by his own forces, his own living conditions and those of his family, to create for himself and those dear to him a field in which they may rightly enjoy not only economic freedom, but political, cultural, and religious freedom as well.

The Christian conscience cannot admit as just a social order which either denies in principle or renders impossible or nugatory in practice, the natural right to property whether over consumptive goods or the means of production.

But neither can it accept those systems which recognize the right to private property according to a completely false concept of it and which are therefore opposed to a true and healthy social order.

Accordingly where, for instance, "Capitalism" is based on such false concepts and arrogates to itself an unlimited right over property, without any subordination to the common good, the Church has condemned it as contrary to the natural law (Reconstruction 1944, 580).

Protection. But this teaching on the right of private property does not mean, evidently, that the Church is the defender of the status quo.

In defending, therefore, the principle of private property, the Church pursues a high ethico-social purpose. She does not intend to defend absolutely and simply the present state of affairs, as if she saw in it the expression of God's will, nor to defend as a matter of principle the rich and the plutocrat against the poor and the indigent. Far from it! Right from the beginning she has been the defender of the oppressed against the tyranny of the powerful, and has always sponsored the just claims of all classes of workers against every injustice. But the Church aims rather at securing that the institution of private property be such as it should be according to the designs of God's wisdom and the dispositions of nature; an element of social order, a necessary pre-supposition to human initiative, an incentive to work to the advantage of life's purpose here and hereafter, and hence of the liberty and the dignity of man, created in the likeness of God, Who, from the beginning, assigned him for his benefit domination over material things (Reconstruction 1944, 581).

Yet when the State brings private ownership into harmony with the needs of the common good, it does not commit a hostile act against private owners but rather does them a friendly service; for it thereby effectively prevents the private possession of goods, which the Author of nature in His most wise providence ordained for the support of human life, from causing intolerable evils and thus rushing to its own destruction; it does not destroy private possessions, but safeguards them; and it does not weaken private property rights, but strengthens them [QUADRAGESIMO ANNO, 49].

It follows from what We have termed the individual and at the same time social character of ownership, that men must consider in this matter not only their own advantage but also the common good. To define these duties in detail when necessity requires and the natural law has not done so, is the function of those in charge of the State. Therefore, public authority under the guiding light always of the natural and divine law, can determine more accurately upon consideration of the true requirements of the common good, what is permitted and what is not permitted to owners in the use of their property. Moreover, Leo XIII wisely taught "that God has left the limits of private possessions to be fixed by the industry of men and institutions of peoples" [RERUM NOVARUM, 14]. That history proves ownership, like other elements of social life, to be not absolutely unchanging, We once declared . . . [QUADRAGESIMO ANNO, 49].

The fact that God gave the whole human race the earth to use and enjoy cannot indeed in any manner serve as an objection against private possessions. For God is said to have given the earth to mankind in common, not because He intended indiscriminate ownership of it by all but because He assigned no part to anyone in ownership, leaving the limits of private possessions to be fixed by the industry of men and the institutions of peoples. Yet, however the earth may be apportioned among private owners, it does not cease to serve the common interest of all, inasmuch as no living being is sustained except by what the fields bring forth. Those who lack resources supply labor, so that it can be truly affirmed that the entire scheme of securing a livelihood consists in the labor which a person expends either on his own land or in some working occupation, the compensation for which is drawn ultimately from no other source than from the varied products of the earth and is exchanged for them [RERUM NOVARUM, 14].

But it will be well to touch here expressly on certain matters of special importance. The capital point is this, that private property ought to be safeguarded by the sovereign power of the State and through the bulwark of its laws. And especially, in view of such a great flaming up of passion at the present time, the masses ought to be kept within the bounds of their moral obligations. For while justice does not oppose our striving for better things, on the other hand, it does forbid anyone to take from another what is his and, in the name of a certain absurd equality, to seize forcibly the property of others; nor does the interest of the common good itself permit this [RERUM NOVARUM, 55].

Right of All. This statement, however, does not infer that there is an unrestricted right of private property, for the right of all men to the use of material goods takes precedence over the right of private property, as Pope Pius XII observes in the following passage:

Every man as a living being gifted with reason has in fact from nature the fundamental right to make use of the material goods of the earth while it is left to the will of man and to the juridical statutes of nations to regulate in greater detail the actuation of this right.

This individual right cannot in any way be suppressed, even by other clear and undisputed rights over material goods.

Undoubtedly the natural order deriving from God demands also private property and the free reciprocal commerce of goods by interchange and gift as well as the functioning of the State as a control over both these institutions. But all this remains subordinate to the natural scope of material goods and cannot emancipate itself from the first and fundamental right which concedes their use to all men; but it should rather serve to make possible the actuation of this right in conformity with its scope (Pentecost, 8).

Woe to him who forgets that a true national society incorporates social justice and demands a just and fitting sharing by all in the goods of the country. Otherwise you understand that the nation would end in a sentimental makeshift, in a nonsensical pretense which would be an excuse for certain groups to withdraw themselves from the sacrifices needed to secure public equilibrium and peace.

And you would then realize how, when national society had lost the nobility given to it by God, internal strife and struggle would become a threat which all might fear (Italian Workers 1943, 4).

Thus the right of private property involves the principle of equitable distribution.

Likewise national economy, as it is the product of men who work together in the community of the State, has no other end than to secure without interruption material conditions in which the individual life of the citizens may fully develop. Where this is secured in a permanent way a people will be in true sense economically rich because the general well-being and consequently the personal right of all to the use of worldly good is thus actuated in conformity with the purpose willed by the Creator.

From this . . . it will be easy for you to conclude that the economic riches of a people do not properly consist in the abundance of goods measured according to a purely and solely material calculation of their worth but in the fact that such an abundance represents and offers really and effectively the material basis sufficient for the proper personal development of its members.

If such a just distribution of goods were not secured or were effected imperfectly, the real scope of national economy would not be attained; for although there were at hand a lucky abundance of goods to dispose of, the people, in not being called upon to share them, would not be economically rich but poor. Suppose, on the other hand, that such a distribution is affected genuinely and permanently and you will see a people, even if it disposes of less goods, making itself economically sound.

These fundamental concepts regarding the riches and poverty of peoples it seems to Us particularly opportune to set before you today when there is a tendency to measure and judge such riches and poverty by balance sheets and by purely quantitative criteria of the need or the redundance of goods. If, instead, the scope of the national economy is correctly considered, then it will become a guide for the efforts of statesmen and peoples and will enlighten them to walk spontaneously along a way which does not call for continual exactions in goods and blood but will give fruits of peace and general welfare (Pentecost, 9-10).

Errors and Abuses. Pope Pius XII carefully clarifies the correct path to take in order to avoid the errors in the denial of the right to private property and, at the other extreme, the abuse of this right.

Others show themselves no less timid and uncertain in the face of that economic system which derives its name from the excessive amassing of private wealth [excessive, or exaggerated, capitalism],* the serious effect of which the Church has never ceased to denounce. The Church has not only indicated the abuses of capital and the right to property promoted and defended by this system, but has insisted just as much that capital and private property must be instruments of production for the benefit of the whole of society and the means of sustaining and defending the freedom and dignity of the human person. . . . This teaching [social teaching of the Church] is the only one that can remedy the evils We have denounced, evils which are so widespread. This teaching unites and perfects the demands of justice and the duties of charity and promotes a social order which does not oppress individuals and isolate them in a blind selfishness but unites everyone in harmonious relations and the bond of fraternal solidarity (Menti Nostrae, 123).

Duties of the State. The State, as has been noted, can act to assure equitable distribution of property. In effect, this may involve supplying employment, exercising the

* Phrase in brackets inserted by translator. The preceding phrasing is a literal translation of the official Latin text. Because the Italian translation appearing in *L'Osservatore Romano* used the word "capitalism" while the Latin did not, the N.C.W.C. News Service requested a precise explanation of the meaning of the Latin phrase. Msgr. Antonio Bacci, secretary of the Vatican Secretariate for Briefs to Princes, said that what was intended by the Latin phrase was "excessive or exaggerated capitalism." Monsignor Bacci heads the Secretariate that is charged with the preparation in Latin of documents committed to it by the Pope [footnote in N.C.W.C. edition of Menti Nostrae].

right of eminent domain, and promoting the welfare of small owners.

The State must take every measure necessary to supply employment, particularly for the heads of families and for the young. To achieve this end demanded by the pressing needs of the common welfare, the wealthy classes must be induced to assume those burdens without which human society cannot be saved nor they themselves remain secure. However, measures taken by the State with this end in view ought to be of such a nature that they will really affect those who actually possess more than their share of capital resources, and who continue to accumulate them to the grievous detriment of others [DIVINI REDEMPTORIS, 75].

The social and economic policy of the future, the controlling power of the State, of local bodies, of professional institutions cannot permanently secure their end, which is the genuine productivity of social life and the normal returns on national economy, except by respecting and safeguarding the vital function of private property in its personal and social values. When the distribution of property is an obstacle to this end— which is not necessarily nor always an outcome of the extension of private inheritance—the State may, in the public interest, intervene by regulating its use or even if it cannot equitably meet the situation in any other way, by decreeing the expropriation of property, giving a suitable indemnity.

For the same purpose small and medium holdings in agriculture, in the arts and trades, in commerce and industry should be guaranteed and promoted; co-operative unions should ensure for them the advantages of big business; where big business even today shows itself more productive, there should be given the possibility of tempering the labor contract with a contract of co-ownership [Encyclical QUADRAGESIMO ANNO].

And it should not be said that technical progress is opposed to such a scheme, and in its irresistible current carries all activity forward toward gigantic business and organizations, before which a social system founded on the private property of individuals must inevitably collapse. No. Technical progress does not determine economic life as a fatal and necessary factor. It has indeed too often yielded timidly to the demands of rapacious, selfish plans calculated to accumulate indefinitely; why should it not then yield also to the necessity of maintaining and ensuring private property for all, that cornerstone of social order? Even technical progress, as a social factor, should not prevail over the general good, but should rather be directed and subordinated to it. (Reconstruction, 1944, 581-582).

The Church defends the right of private property, a right she considers fundamentally inalienable. But she insists also on the need for a more just distribution of property and deplores the unnatural social situation in which an enormous mass of impoverished people live beside a small group of very rich and privileged (Spanish Employers and Workers, 707).

Chapter XIV

Dignity of Labor; the Family; International Order

DIGNITY OF LABOR

Value of Labor. All labor, whether it is pleasurable in itself, or whether it is "monotonous and difficult," has a dignity and nobility to which the Popes have repeatedly called attention. For example:

. . . labor, while often causing sad and fretful fatigue, is nevertheless in itself beautiful and ennobling. Because it is productive, it continues the work begun by the Creator and represents the full collaboration of each one for the benefit of all. Such a thought should be sufficient to make all work agreeable, even the most monotonous and difficult (Nobility, 564).

Labor's Function in the Divine Plan. "For the Christian, professional work is a manner of serving God." (Bank of Italy, 331).

Even if, with the passing years, professional work should become monotonous, or if, by obedience to the law of God, it should weigh on one like a restrictive and too heavy load, it will always remain nonetheless for you, Christians, one of the

174

most important means of satisfaction, one of the most efficacious ways of conforming yourselves to the Divine Will, and
thus of meriting heaven.

A Christian cannot consider his work in any other way. If
there is today so much discontent, so much indifference and
irresponsibility, that is because a clear and true concept of
the Christian value of work no longer exists, or if it does exist,
is no longer a living force in souls (Bank of Italy, 331-332).

You, Farmers, form with your families a working-community. With your companions and associates also you form a
working-community. Finally, with all the professional or vocational groups of the whole people you constitute one big
working-community. This is in accordance with the order of
God and of nature: it is the true Catholic concept of work.
Thus men are brought together to work for the needs of the
people and perfect themselves by their united efforts, to the
honor of their Creator and Redeemer (Farmer, 446).

Nor is it to be thought that gainful occupations are thereby
belittled or judged less consonant with human dignity; on
the contrary, we are taught to recognize in them with reverence the manifest will of the Divine Creator Who placed man
upon the earth to work it and use it in a multitude of ways for
his needs [QUADRAGESIMO ANNO, 136].

Labor, as Our Predecessor explained well in his Encyclical,
is not a mere commodity. On the contrary, the worker's human dignity in it must be recognized. It therefore cannot be
bought and sold like a commodity [QUADRAGESIMO ANNO, 83].

For work is not only, for every man, a means of decent
livelihood, but it is the means through which all those manifold powers and faculties with which nature, training, and art
have endowed the dignity of the human personality, find their
necessary expression, and this with a certain natural comeli-
ness (Easter, 128).

Christ Himself raised labor even "to a sublime and supreme height":

Our Redeemer entered this world in the guise of a humble worker, a son of labor, and destined to become a workman Himself. When, moreover, He presented Himself to the world to begin His public life, His Divine Apostolate, He was called the carpenter's son, the workman's son.

All that indicates clearly enough the place that workers occupy in the Redemption, and in the Heart of the Redeemer. Jesus, coming into the world, took His place among them; this is the truth, and work that has now become your tribulation on account of its cessation, has been—let us not forget—raised to a sublime and supreme height; the height of God Himself, because it became the work of a Man-God, a thing of God; herein is to be found not only the exaltation of work, but its very godliness (Pilgrims, 21-22).

THE FAMILY

Position of the Family. The family has been referred to by Pope Pius XII as one of "the two master columns of society" in the "inner structure" of that society (Society, 200).

It is precisely in these years of economic and social upheaval that religious and eternal values have powerfully demonstrated their absolute indestructibility: God and His natural law; Christ and His Kingdom of truth and grace; the Christian family, always the same and always the backbone and measure of the economic and public order; the sweet, sure hope of the beyond, of the resurrection and eternal life (Catholic Action, 54).

Wherefore, assuming, of course, that those limits be observed which are fixed by its immediate purpose, the family assuredly possesses rights, at least equal with those of civil society, in respect to choosing and employing the things necessary for its protection and its just liberty. We say "at least equal" because, inasmuch as domestic living together is prior both in thought and in fact to uniting into a polity, it follows that its rights and duties are also prior and more in conformity with nature [RERUM NOVARUM, 20].

Family Living Wage. Subsistence is among these rights and hence the right of a family living wage.

In the first place, the worker must be paid a wage sufficient to support him and his family. That the rest of the family should also contribute to the common support, according to the capacity of each, is certainly right, as can be observed especially in the families of farmers, but also in the families of many craftsmen and small shopkeepers. But to abuse the years of childhood and the limited strength of women is grossly wrong. Mothers, concentrating on household duties, should work primarily in the home or in its immediate vicinity. It is an intolerable abuse, and to be abolished at all cost, for mothers on account of the father's low wage to be forced to engage in gainful occupations outside the home to the neglect of their proper cares and duties, especially the training of children. Every effort must therefore be made that fathers of families receive a wage large enough to meet ordinary family needs adequately. But if this cannot always be done under existing circumstances, social justice demands that changes be introduced as soon as possible whereby such a wage will be assured to every adult workingman. It will not be out of place here to render merited praise to all, who, with a wise and useful purpose, have tried and tested various ways of adjusting the pay for work to family burdens in such a way that, as these increase, the former may be raised and indeed, if the contingency arises, there may be enough to meet extraordinary needs [QUADRAGESIMO ANNO, 71].

A man's work ought to give to him and his family a sufficiency of daily bread. That sufficiency is not something which is added in a sort of extrinsic fashion; it is intrinsically connected with professional work according to the designs of God (Bank of Italy, 332).

A Grave Responsibility. The gravity and urgency inhering in the principle of a just wage is spelled out in unmistakable terms:

. . . every effort must be made to bring about that which Our predecessor Leo XIII, of happy memory, has already insisted upon, namely, that in the State such economic and social methods should be adopted as will enable every head of a family to earn as much as, according to his station in life, is necessary for himself, his wife, and for the rearing of his children, for "the labourer is worthy of his hire." To deny this, or to make light of what is equitable, is a grave injustice and is placed among the greatest sins by Holy Writ; nor is it lawful to fix such a scanty wage as will be insufficient for the upkeep of the family in the circumstances in which it is placed [CASTI CONNUBII, p. 42].

. . . if legislation is to play its part in the pacification of the community, it must prevent the worker, who is or will be a father of a family, from being condemned to an economic dependence and slavery which is irreconcilable with his rights as a person (Christmas 1942, 12).

There are many factors which must contribute to a greater diffusion of property. But the principal one always will be a just salary . . . a just salary and a better distribution of natural wealth constitute two of the most impelling demands in the social program of the Church (Spanish Employers and Workers, 707).

In the following statements Pope Pius XII explains the basis upon which the gravity of responsibility rests:

If it is true that the best and most natural means of satisfying this obligation [to meet the demands of necessity and decent comfort] is to increase available goods through a healthy development of production, it is still necessary, in pursuing this effort, to have care to distribute justly the fruit of the labor of all (Semaines 1952, 12).

The Pope points out that inequitable distribution defeats the purpose of national economy:

If such a just distribution of goods were not secured or were effected imperfectly, the real scope of national economy would not be attained; for although there were at hand a lucky abundance of goods to dispose of, the people, in not being called upon to share them, would not be economically rich but poor. Suppose, on the other hand, that such a distribution is affected genuinely and permanently and you will see a people, even if it disposes of less goods, making itself economically sound (Pentecost, 9-10).

Pope Pius XII explains further:

This basic distribution is originally and normally brought about by virtue of the continuous dynamism of the social economic process of which We have spoken, and this is for a great many men the source of their wages as recompense for their work.

But we must not overlook that, from the point of view of the national economy, these wages correspond to the income of the worker (Semaines 1952, 12).

His Holiness then points out a principle of co-operation which underlies the Industry Council Plan:

Managers of industry and workers are here co-operators in a common task: both of them are called upon to derive their livelihood from the actual and total profits of the economy. Looked at from this point of view, their mutual relations do not in any way imply that the one should merely serve the other (Semaines 1952, 12).

It should be kept in mind that the right to proper re-muneration for work stems from the dignity of a human person and the purpose of earthly goods.

To receive one's wage is a prerogative of the personal dig-nity of anyone who makes his productive contribution in one form or another, as employer or laborer, towards the output of the nation's economy (Employers, 445-446).

Reason for Living Wage. Pope Leo XIII shows, through the factor of necessity, why a living wage must be paid even though the worker—under duress—might agree to accept less.

We shall now touch upon a matter of very great importance, and one which must be correctly understood in order to avoid falling into error on one side or the other. We are told that free consent fixes the amount of a wage; that therefore the employer, after paying the wage agreed to, would seem to have discharged his obligation and not to owe anything more; that only then would injustice be done if either the employer should refuse to pay the whole amount of the wage, or the worker should refuse to perform all the work to which he had committed himself; and that in these cases, but in no others, is it proper for the public authority to intervene to safeguard the rights of each party.

An impartial judge would not assent readily or without reservation to this reasoning, because it is not complete in all respects; one factor to be considered, and one of the greatest importance, is missing. To work is to expend one's energy for the purpose of securing the things necessary for the various needs of life and especially for its preservation. "In the sweat of thy face shalt thou eat bread" (Gen. 3:19). Accordingly, in man labor has two marks, as it were, implanted by nature, so that it is truly *personal*, because work energy inheres in the person and belongs completely to him by whom it is expended and for whose use it is destined by nature; and, secondly, that it is *necessary*, because man has need of the fruit of his labors to preserve his life, and nature itself, which must be most strictly obeyed, commands him to preserve it. If labor should be considered only under the aspect that it is personal, there is no doubt that it would be entirely in the worker's power to set the amount of the agreed wage at too low a figure. For inasmuch as he performs work by his own free will, he can also by his own free will be satisfied with either a paltry wage for his work or even with none at all. But this matter must be judged far differently, if with the factor of *personality* we combine the factor of *necessity*, from which indeed the former is separable in thought but not in reality. In fact, to preserve one's life is a duty common to all individuals, and to neglect this duty is a crime. Hence arises necessarily the right of securing things to sustain life, and only a wage earned by his labor gives a poor man the means to acquire these things [RERUM NOVARUM, 61, 62].

Other statements on the living wage are to be found under "Social Justice," supra, pp. 131 ff.

INTERNATIONAL ORDER

World Community. If the Industry Council Plan is ever to be extended to the international level, it can be only in an international society which constitutes a true "family of nations."

The Catholic doctrine on the State and civil society has always been based on the principle that, in keeping with the will of God, the nations form together a community with a common aim and common duties. Even when the proclamation of this principle and its practical consequences gave rise to violent reactions, the Church denied her assent to the erroneous concept of an absolutely autonomous sovereignty divested of all social obligations.

The Catholic Christian, persuaded that every man is his neighbor and that every nation is a member, with equal rights, of the family of nations, co-operates wholeheartedly in those generous efforts whose beginnings might be meager and which frequently encounter strong opposition and obstacles, but which aim at saving individual States from narrowness of a self-centered mentality (Christmas 1948, 18-19).

Actually, rivalries and enmities exist, and Pope Pius XI put his finger on the cause.

And it is from this intemperance of desire, sheltering itself under an appearance of public good or love of country, that come the rivalries and enmities that We see between nations. Those who are carried away by such considerations assuredly forget, not only that all the peoples, as parts of the universal human family, are joined together as brothers among themselves, and that other nations too have the right to live and prosper, but also that it is never lawful or expedient to separate what is useful from what is right. *For Justice exalteth a nation, but sin maketh nations miserable;* advantages gained for the family, State, or public power to the detriment of others may seem great and magnificent achievements, but Saint Augustine shows that they are not lasting and always carry with them fear of disaster: they are a bright joy as brittle as glass accompanied by the haunting fear of a sudden break (Saint Augustine: *De Civitate Dei,* lib. iv, c.3) [UBI ARCANO DEI, pp. 302-303].

Right order of Christian charity does not disapprove of lawful love of country and a sentiment of justifiable nationalism. . . . If however, egoism, abusing this love of country and exaggerating this sentiment of nationalism, insinuates itself into the relations between people and people, there is no excess that will not seem justified . . . [CARITATE CHRISTI COMPULSI, pp. 5-6].

It is essential that the hate, the diffidence, the stimuli of an extreme nationalism should give way to the growth of wise counsels, the flowering of peaceful designs, to serenity in the exchange of views and to mutual brotherly comprehension (Name Day 1945, 456-457).

And how will all this [tranquillity of order in union with the Prince of Peace] come about except through the continuous, enlightening, and strengthening action of the grace of Christ on the minds and hearts of citizens and statesmen, so that in all human relationships they recognize and pursue the purposes of the Creator, so that they strive to enlist the collaboration of individuals and nations for effecting these purposes, so that within as well as among nations they practice social justice and charity? (Christmas 1951, 252-53).

Brotherhood in Fatherhood of God. Unity of mankind extends to the international level because of the brotherhood of man in the Fatherhood of God. Disputes and injustices between nations are a violation of this unity.

A disposition, in fact, of the divinely sanctioned natural order divides the human race into social groups, nations or States, which are mutually independent in organization and in the direction of their internal life. But for all that, the human race is bound together by reciprocal ties, moral and juridical, into a great commonwealth directed to the good of all nations and ruled by special laws which protect its unity and promote its prosperity.

Now no one can fail to see how the claim to absolute autonomy for the State stands in open opposition to this natural way that is inherent in man—nay, denies it utterly—and therefore leaves the stability of international relations at the mercy of the will of rulers, while it destroys the possibility of true union and fruitful collaboration directed to the general good [SUMMI PONTIFICATUS, 65-66].

The idea which credits the State with unlimited authority is not simply an error harmful to the internal life of nations, to their prosperity, and to the larger and well-ordered increase in their well-being, but likewise it injures the relations between peoples, for it breaks the unity of supra-national society, robs the law of nations of its foundation and vigor, leads to violation of others' rights and impedes agreement and peaceful intercourse [SUMMI PONTIFICATUS, 64].

Socio-Economic Implications. From these principles it follows that

The progress and the extent of urgent social reforms depend on the economic possibilities of single nations. It is only through an intelligent and generous sharing of forces between the strong and the weak that it will be possible to effect a universal pacification in such wise as not to leave behind centers of conflagration and infection from which new disasters may come (Christmas 1942, 17).

First: Within the limits of a new order founded on moral principles there is no room for violation of the freedom, integrity, and security of other states, no matter what may be their territorial extension or their capacity for defense. If it is inevitable that the powerful states should, by reason of their greater potentialities and their power, play leading roles in the formation of economic groups, comprising not only themselves but smaller and weaker states as well, it is nevertheless indispensable that in the interests of the common good they, and all others, respect the rights of those smaller states to political freedom, to economic development, and to the adequate protection, in the case of conflicts between nations, of that neutrality which is theirs according to the natural as well as international law. In this way, and in this way only, shall they be able to obtain a fitting share of the common good and assure the material and spiritual welfare of the peoples concerned.

. . . .

Thirdly: Within the limits of a new order founded on moral principles there is no place for that cold and calculating egoism which tends to hoard economic resources and materials destined for the use of all, to such an extent that the nations less favored by nature are not permitted access to them. In this regard, it is a source of great consolation to see admitted the necessity of a participation of all in the natural riches of the earth even on the part of those nations which, in the fulfillment of this principle, belong to the category of givers and not to that of receivers. It is, however, in conformity with the principles of equity that a solution to a question so vital to the world economy should be arrived at methodically, and in easy stages with a necessary guarantee, always drawing useful lessons from the omissions and mistakes of the past. If, in the future peace, this point were not to be courageously dealt with, there would remain in the relations between people a deep and far-reaching root blossoming forth into bitter dissensions and burning jealousies, which would lead eventually to new conflicts (Christmas 1941, 757-758).

Unity and co-operation should be applied in regard to movement of peoples.

When this happens [recognition of the right of the family to a vital space], emigration attains its natural scope, as experience often shows; We mean the more favorable distribution of men on the earth's surface suitable to colonies of agricultural workers; that surface which God created and prepared for the use of all.

If the two parties, those who agree to leave their native land and those who agree to admit the newcomers, remain anxious to eliminate as far as possible all obstacles to the birth and growth of real confidence between the country of emigration and that of immigration, all those affected by such a transference of people and places will profit by the transaction: the families will receive a plot of ground which will be native land for them in the true sense of the word. The thickly inhabited countries will be relieved, and their people will acquire new friends in foreign countries; and the states which receive the emigrants will acquire industrious citizens. In this way the nations which give and those which receive will both contribute to the increased welfare of man and the progress of human culture (Pentecost, 13-14).

World trade should be determined by these same principles.

In international trade-relations let all means be sedulously employed for the removal of those artificial barriers to economic life which are the effects of distrust and hatred. All must remember that the peoples of the earth form but one family in God [DIVINI REDEMPTORIS, 76].

The relations between agriculture and industry within the single national economies, and of those latter with the economy of other nations, the manner and extent that each nation is to share in the world market—all these difficult problems present themselves today afresh and under aspects different from those of previous times. Upon their rational solution depends the productivity of the several nations, and consequently the welfare of individuals as well; for it is clear that there can never be sufficient distribution where there is not sufficient production (Name Day 1948, 485).

Above all, there must be victory over the evil principle of utility as the basis and rule of what is right in economic life. This means victory over those occasions of conflict which arise from glaring disparities, maintained at times by compulsion, in the world economy. It means victory over the spirit of cold egoism, so as to bring about that sincere solidarity, both juridic and economic, which implies fraternal collaboration, according to the precepts of the divine law, among nations assured of their autonomy and freedom. Faith in Christ and observance of His commandments of love alone can bring about such a salutary victory (Exchange, 423).

The Sovereign Pontiffs thus outline the principles and problems involved in adequate and equitable productivity and distribution of resources, access to markets by means of fair-trade practices and economic co-operation among nations, and respect for the rights of all States, large and small. These principles can be perceived correctly only in the perspective of the true nature of man and society and the State as a necessary form of society performing functions proper to its purpose. The solution of these problems in the light of these principles would be the object of the Industry Councils established on a local, regional, national, and international basis.

Chapter XV

Conclusion

THE PRINCIPLES discussed in this book are basic, directly or indirectly, to a successful system of industry councils. Machinery of organization is necessary; but without the quickening spirit of vivifying principles functioning throughout the system, all efforts at effective organization would be futile. It is generally recognized that the process of building up such a system must be a gradual one; that is, no blueprint can be successfully imposed by government fiat. As Pope Pius XII says, reform must come about by evolution, not revolution.

Salvation and justice are not to be found in revolution but in an evolution through concord. Violence has ever achieved only destruction, not construction; the kindling of passions, not their pacification; the accumulation of hate and destruction, not the reconciliation of the contending parties. And it has reduced men and parties to the difficult task of building slowly after sad experience on the ruins of discord.

It is only a progressive and prudent evolution, full of courage and in conformity with nature, enlightened and guided by the Christian laws of justice and equity, that can lead to the fulfillment of the honorable desires and needs of the worker. Not to destroy them, but to build and consolidate; not to abolish private property, the foundation of family stability, but to work for its extension as the reward of the conscientious toil of every working man and woman, so that little by little may be diminished that mass of uneasy and rash people who— sometimes from taciturn despair, at others through broad instinct—allow themselves to be carried off by false doctrines or by the clever tricks of agitators who are bereft of all moral sense; not to dissipate private capital, but to promote its regulation under careful control as a means and help toward securing and increasing the genuine welfare of the whole people; not to restrain nor to give preference exclusively to industry, but to procure its harmonious marriage to handicraft and agriculture, which exploits the multifarious and necessary production of the nation's soil; not to aim in the use of technical progress solely at the maximum profit, but also to avail one's self of the advantages which come from it, in order to better the personal conditions of the worker, to make his work less arduous and difficult, and to consolidate the bonds which hold his family together in the place where he dwells, in the work by which he lives; not to aim at making the lives of individuals depend entirely on the whims of the State, but to procure rather that the State, whose duty it is to promote the common good, may, through social institutions such as insurance and social security societies, supply support and complete all that helps to strengthen workers' associations, and especially the fathers and mothers of families who are earning a livelihood for themselves and their dependents through work (Italian Workers 1943, 4-5).

Assuredly the reduction to practice and application of this doctrine [social doctrine of the Church] cannot be the work of a day. Its realization requires of all participants in the process a discretion born of insight and foresight, a strong dose of good sense and good will. It demands of them especially a radical reaction against the temptation to seek each one's own advantage at the expense of the other partners—whatever be the nature and form of their participation—and to the detriment of the common welfare. It calls finally for unselfishness of a sort which can only be instilled by an authentic Christian virtue, sustained and aided by the grace of God (Employers, 447-448).

Pope Pius XI summarizes the principles discussed by the Sovereign Pontiffs in their encyclicals and allocutions, the statements of which have been collected in the present volume as clarifications of the goal the Industry Council Plan seeks to achieve.

. . . We have shown that the means of saving the world of today from the lamentable ruin into which amoral liberalism has plunged us, are neither the class-struggle nor terror, nor yet the autocratic abuse of State power, but rather the infusion of social justice and the sentiment of Christian love into the social-economic order. We have indicated how a sound prosperity is to be restored according to the true principles of a sane corporative system which respects the proper hierarchic structure of society; and how all the occupational groups should be fused into a harmonious unity inspired by the principle of the common good. And the genuine and chief function of public and civil authority consists precisely in the efficacious furthering of this harmony and co-ordination of all social forces [DIVINI REDEMPTORIS, 32].

The general principles also are summarized in QUADRA-GESIMO ANNO.

All experts in social problems are seeking eagerly a structure so fashioned in accordance with the norms of reason that it can lead economic life back to sound and right order. But this order, which We Ourselves ardently long for and with all Our efforts promote, will be wholly defective and incomplete unless all the activities of men harmoniously unite to imitate and attain, in so far as it lies within human strength, the marvelous unity of the Divine plan. We mean that perfect order which the Church with great force and power preaches and which right human reason itself demands, that all things be directed to God as the first and supreme end of all created activity, and that all created good under God be considered as mere instruments to be used only in so far as they conduce to the attainment of the supreme end [QUADRAGESIMO ANNO, 136].

Key to Documents Cited

Numbers in parentheses following quotations from works other than encyclicals refer to pages. For encyclicals, numbers refer to paragraphs (unless page is indicated). Encyclicals are set off in small capital letters. See pp. 197 ff. for complete bibliographical data.

Action	Pius XII. Address to Men of Catholic Action of Italy, September 7, 1947.
AD BEATISSIMI	Benedict XV. AD BEATISSIMI, November 1, 1914.
AU MILIEU DES SOLLICITUDES	Leo XIII. AU MILIEU DES SOLLICITUDES, February 16, 1892.
AUSPICIA QUAEDAM	Pius XII. AUSPICIA QUAEDAM, May 1, 1948.
Bank of Italy	Pius XII. Allocution to Directors and Employees of the Bank of Italy, April 25, 1950.
Belgian Workers	Pius XII. Allocution to Members of the Christian Workers' Movement of Belgium, September 11, 1949.
Businessmen	Pius XII. Address to Delegates of the World Congress of Chambers of Commerce, April 27, 1950.
CARITATE CHRISTI COMPULSI	Pius XI. CARITATE CHRISTI COMPULSI, May 3, 1932.
CASTI CONNUBII	Pius XI. CASTI CONNUBII, December 31, 1930.
Catholic Action	Pius XII. Address to Members of Catholic Action, September 12, 1948.
Christian Workers	Pius XII. Address to the Young Christian Workers, March 21, 1949.
Christmas 1940	Pius XII. Christmas Message, December 24, 1940.

192

Christmas 1941	Pius XII. Christmas Message, December 24, 1941.
Christmas 1942	Pius XII. Christmas Message, December 24, 1942.
Christmas 1943	Pius XII. Christmas Message, December 24, 1943.
Christmas 1944	Pius XII. Christmas Message, December 24, 1944.
Christmas 1948	Pius XII. Christmas Message, December 23, 1948.
Christmas 1949	Pius XII. Christmas Message, December 23, 1949.
Christmas 1950	Pius XII. Christmas Message, December 23, 1950.
Christmas 1951	Pius XII. Christmas Eve Address, December 24, 1951.
DIUTURNUM ILLUD	Leo XIII. DIUTURNUM ILLUD, June 29, 1881.
DIVINI ILLIUS MAGISTRI	Pius XI. DIVINI ILLIUS MAGISTRI, December 31, 1929.
DIVINI REDEMP-TORIS	Pius XI. DIVINI REDEMPTORIS, March 19, 1937.
Easter	Pius XII. Easter Sermon on Peace, April 9, 1939.
Employers	Pius XII. Address to Catholic Employers, May 7, 1949.
Exchange	Pius XII. Address to Congress of International Exchange, March 7, 1948.
Farmer	Pius XII. Address to the Italian Farmers' Federation, November 15, 1946.
GRAVES DE COM-MUNI	Leo XIII. GRAVES DE COMMUNI, January 18, 1901.
IL FERMO PROPO-SITO	Pius X. IL FERMO PROPOSITO, June 11, 1905.
IMMORTALE DEI	Leo XIII. IMMORTALE DEI, November 1, 1885.
INSCRUTABILI	Leo XIII. INSCRUTABILI, April 21, 1878.
International Labor	Pius XII. Address to the International Labor Organization, July 16, 1947.
Italian Employers	Pius XII. Address to Italian Catholic Association of Employers, January 31, 1952.

Italian Workers 1943	Pius XII. Address to Italian Workers, June 13, 1943.
Italian Workers 1945	Pius XII. Address to Italian Workers, March 11, 1945.
Italian Workers 1948	Pius XII. Address to Italian Workers, June 29, 1948.
Jurists	Pius XII. Address to Members of the Convention of the Union of Italian Catholic Jurists, November 6, 1949.
Katholikentag	Pius XII. Address to Members of the Austrian National Catholic Convention (Katholikentag), September 14, 1952.
Labor's Dignity	Pius XII. Address to Members of Fiat Automotive Plant, October 31, 1948.
LAETITIAE SANCTAE	Leo XIII. LAETITIAE SANCTAE, September 8, 1892.
Law	Pius XII. Address to Members of First International Private Law Congress, July 15, 1950.
LIBERTAS PRAE-STANTISSIMUM	Leo XIII. LIBERTAS PRAESTANTISSIMUM, June 20, 1888.
Medical Congress	Pius XII. Address to the First International Congress on the Histopathology of the Nervous System, September 14, 1952.
Menti Nostrae	Pius XII. Menti Nostrae, September 23, 1950.
MIT BRENNENDER SORGE	Pius XI. MIT BRENNENDER SORGE, March 14, 1937.
MYSTICI CORPORIS CHRISTI	Pius XII. MYSTICI CORPORIS CHRISTI, June 29, 1943.
Name Day 1945	Pius XII. Address to Sacred College of Cardinals, June 2, 1945.
Name Day 1947	Pius XII. Allocution to the Sacred College of Cardinals, June 2, 1947.
Name Day 1948	Pius XII. Allocution to the Sacred College of Cardinals, June 2, 1948.
Nobility	Pius XII. Address to Workers of Civita Castellana, March 27, 1949.
OPTATISSIMA PAX	Pius XII. OPTATISSIMA PAX, December 18, 1947.
Peace	Pius XII. Allocution to the Sacred College of Cardinals, June 1, 1946.

Pentecost	Pius XII. Address to the World on the Feast of Pentecost, June 1, 1941.
Pilgrims	Pius XI. Address to Pilgrims, 1933.
Problem	Pius XII. Radio Address to the German Catholic Congress, Bochum, September 4, 1949.
Production	Pius XII. Address to Delegates to Catholic International Congresses for Social Studies and Social Action, June 3, 1950.
QUADRAGESIMO ANNO	Pius XI. QUADRAGESIMO ANNO, May 15, 1931.
QUOD APOSTOLICI MUNERIS	Leo XIII. QUOD APOSTOLICI MUNERIS, December 28, 1878.
Reconstruction 1944	Pius XII. Address on Fifth Anniversary of the Outbreak of War, September 1, 1944.
RERUM NOVARUM	Leo XIII. RERUM NOVARUM, May 15, 1891.
Rural Problems	Pius XII. Address to the First International Catholic Congress on Rural Problems, July 2, 1951.
SAPIENTIAE CHRISTIANAE	Leo XIII. SAPIENTIAE CHRISTIANAE, January 10, 1890.
Semaines 1945	Pius XII. To Semaines Sociales de France, July 14, 1945.
Semaines 1946	Pius XII. To Semaines Sociales de France, July 10, 1946.
Semaines 1947	Pius XII. To Semaines Sociales de France, July 18, 1947.
Semaines 1952	Pius XII. Letter to Charles Flory, President of Semaines Sociales de France, July 7, 1952.
SERTUM LAETITIAE	Pius XII. SERTUM LAETITIAE, November 1, 1939.
Sillon	Pius X. Letter to the French Archbishops and Bishops (Le Sillon), August 25, 1910.
Society	Pius XII. Allocution to the College of Cardinals, February 20, 1946.
Spanish Employers and Workers	Pius XII. Address to Spanish Catholic Employers and Workers, March 11, 1951.
SUMMI MAERORIS	Pius XII. SUMMI MAERORIS, July 19, 1950.
SUMMI PONTIFICATUS	Pius XII. SUMMI PONTIFICATUS, October 20, 1939.

Truman   Pius XII. To President Truman, August 26,
                        1947.
UBI ARCANO DEI   Pius XI. UBI ARCANO DEI, December 23, 1922.
Women   Pius XII. Allocution to Italian Women, October
                        21, 1945.
World Federalism   Pius XII. Discourse to Fourth Congress of the
                        World Movement for World Federal Gov-
                        ernment, April 6, 1951.

Bibliography of Papal Documents

Encyclicals

Leo XIII

INSCRUTABILI, April 21, 1878. Husslein, Joseph. *Social Wellsprings*. Vol. I. Milwaukee: Bruce, 1940.

QUOD APOSTOLICI MUNERIS, December 28, 1878. Husslein. *Social Wellsprings*. Vol. I.

DIUTURNUM ILLUD, June 29, 1881. New York: The Paulist Press, 1942.

IMMORTALE DEI, November 1, 1885. New York: The Paulist Press, 1941.

LIBERTAS PRAESTANTISSIMUM, June 20, 1888. Husslein. *Social Wellsprings*. Vol. I.

SAPIENTIAE CHRISTIANAE, January 10, 1890. Husslein. *Social Wellsprings*. Vol. I.

RERUM NOVARUM, May 15, 1891. Washington: National Catholic Welfare Conference.

AU MILIEU DES SOLLICITUDES, February 16, 1892. *Great Encyclical Letters of Pope Leo XIII*. New York: Benziger, 1903.

LAETITIAE SANCTAE, September 8, 1892. Husslein. *Social Wellsprings*. Vol. I.

GRAVES DE COMMUNI, January 18, 1901. *The Pope and the People*. London: Catholic Truth Society, 1929.

Pius X

II FERMO PROPOSITO, June 11, 1905. *The Pope and the People*.

Benedict XV

AD BEATISSIMI, November 1, 1914. *The Pope and the People*.

Pius XI

UBI ARCANO DEI, December 23, 1922. *The Pope Speaks.* New York: Harcourt Brace, 1940.

DIVINI ILLIUS MAGISTRI, December 31, 1929. Washington: National Catholic Welfare Conference.

CASTI CONNUBII, December 31, 1930. Washington: National Catholic Welfare Conference.

QUADRAGESIMO ANNO, May 15, 1931. Washington: National Catholic Welfare Conference.

CARITATE CHRISTI COMPULSI, May 3, 1932. Washington: National Catholic Welfare Conference.

MIT BRENNENDER SORGE, March 14, 1937. Washington: National Catholic Welfare Conference.

DIVINI REDEMPTORIS, March 19, 1937. Washington: National Catholic Welfare Conference.

Pius XII

SUMMI PONTIFICATUS, October 20, 1939. Washington: National Catholic Welfare Conference.

SERTUM LAETITIAE, November 1, 1939. Washington: National Catholic Welfare Conference.

MYSTICI CORPORIS CHRISTI, June 29, 1943. Washington: National Catholic Welfare Conference.

OPTATISSIMA PAX, December 18, 1947. *The Catholic Mind,* XLVI (February, 1948), 65-67.

AUSPICIA QUAEDAM, May 1, 1948. *The Catholic Mind,* XLVI (July, 1948), 417-420.

SUMMI MAERORIS, July 19, 1950. *The Catholic Mind,* XLVIII (October, 1950), 628-630.

Other Pronouncements

Pius X

Letter to the French Archbishops and Bishops (Le Sillon), August 25, 1910. *American Catholic Quarterly Review,* XXXV (October, 1910), 693-711.

Pius XI

Address to a Pilgrimage of Four Hundred Unemployed Men, 1933. *The Catholic Mind,* XXXII (January 22, 1934), 21-27.

Pius XII

Easter Sermon on Peace, April 9, 1939. *The Pope Speaks.* 126-133.

"Conditions for a New World Order," Christmas Message to the Sacred College of Cardinals and to the World, December 24, 1940. *The Catholic Mind,* XXXIX (January 8, 1941), 1-6.

La Solennita della Pentecoste. "The Social Question in the New Order," Address to the World on the Feast of Pentecost, June 1, 1941. *The Catholic Mind,* XXXIX (June 8, 1941), 1-16.

Christmas Message, December 24, 1941. Koenig, Harry C. *Principles for Peace.* Milwaukee: Bruce, 1943.

Christmas Message, December 24, 1942. Washington: National Catholic Welfare Conference.

Address to Italian Workers, June 13, 1943. *The Catholic Mind,* XLI (July, 1943), 1-9.

Christmas Message, December 24, 1943. *The Catholic Mind,* XLII (February, 1944), 65-76.

"Reconstruction of the World on a True Christian Foundation," Address delivered on the Fifth Anniversary of the Outbreak of War in Europe, September 1, 1944. *The Catholic Mind,* XLII (October, 1944), 577-586.

Christmas Message, December 24, 1944. *The Catholic Mind,* XLIII (February, 1945), 65-77.

Address to the Members of the Christian Associations of Italian Workers, March 11, 1945. *Catholic Action,* XXVII (June, 1945), 5, 22.

"Nazism and Peace," Address to the Sacred College of Cardinals on the Feast of Saint Eugene, June 2, 1945. *The Catholic Mind,* XLIII (August, 1945), 449-457.

To Semaines Sociales de France, July 14, 1945. *The Catholic Mind,* XLIII (October, 1945), 618-619.

"Woman's Duties in Social and Political Life," Allocution to Italian Women, October 21, 1945. *The Catholic Mind,* XLIII (December, 1945), 705-716.

"The Church—Foundation of Society," Allocution to the Sacred College of Cardinals, February 20, 1946. *The Catholic Mind,* XLIV (April, 1946), 193-203.

"On Peace and Liberty," Allocution to the Sacred College of Cardinals, June 1, 1946. *The Catholic Mind,* XLIV (August, 1946), 449-456.

To Charles Flory, President of Semaines Sociales de France, July 10, 1946. *American Ecclesiastical Review,* CXXII (January, 1950), 21.

"The Life of the Farmer," Address delivered to the Italian Farmers' Federation, November 15, 1946. *The Catholic Mind,* XLVIII (July, 1950), 446.

"The Way to True Peace," Allocution to the Sacred College of Cardinals on the Feast of Saint Eugene, June 2, 1947. *Catholic Action,* XXIX (July, 1947), 19-21.

"The Rights of Workers," Address to the American Delegates to the International Labor Organization Conference at Geneva, July 16, 1947. *The Catholic Mind,* XLV (December, 1947), 711-712.

To Semaines Sociales de France, July 18, 1947. *The Catholic Mind,* XLV (November, 1947), 681-684.

To President Truman, August 26, 1947. *The Catholic Mind,* XLV (November, 1947), 653-655.

"Now Is the Time for Action," Address to the Men of Catholic Action of Italy on the Twenty-fifth Anniversary of Its Foundation, September 7, 1947. *The Catholic Mind,* XLV (November, 1947), 641-648.

"Christian Principles of International Trade," Address to the Congress of International Exchange, March 7, 1948. *The Catholic Mind,* XLVI (July, 1948), 421-424.

Allocution to the Sacred College of Cardinals on the Feast of Saint Eugene, June 2, 1948. *The Catholic Mind,* XLVI (August, 1948), 481-488.

"Problems of Italian Workers," Address to Italian Workers, Members of ACLI, Workers' Sector of Italian Catholic Action, June 29, 1948. *The Catholic Mind,* XLVI (October, 1948), 609-616.

"Challenge to Young Men," Address to Members of Italian Catholic Action and Representatives of Fifty-two Other Nations, September 12, 1948. *The Catholic Mind,* XLVII (January, 1949), 51-55.

"Labor's Dignity and Freedom," Address to Representatives of Labor, Management and Catholic Action of Fiat Automotive Plant of Turin, Italy, October 31, 1948. *The Catholic Mind,* XLVII (May, 1949), 303-305.

Christmas Message, December 23, 1948. *Catholic Action,* XXXI (January, 1949), 3, 18-20.

Address to the Young Christian Workers, Letter to Reverend Joseph Cardijn on Celebration of the Twenty-fifth Anniversary of YCW, March 21, 1949. *The Catholic Mind,* XLVII (August, 1949), 508-509.

"Nobility of Work," Address to Workers in Ceramics from Civita Castellana, Italy, March 27, 1949. *The Catholic Mind,* XLVII (September, 1949), 564-565.

Address to the Ninth International Congress of the International Union of Catholic Employers, May 7, 1949. *The Catholic Mind,* XLVII (July, 1949), 445-448.

"The Social Problem," Radio Address to the German Catholic Congress, Bochum, September 4, 1949. *The Catholic Mind,* XLVII (November, 1949), 701-704.

"On Workers' Organization," Allocution to Members of the Christian Workers' Movement of Belgium, September 11, 1949. *The Catholic Mind,* XLVIII (January, 1950), 58-61.

"Duties of Catholic Jurists," Address to Members of the First National Convention of the Union of Italian Catholic Jurists, November 6, 1949. *The Catholic Mind,* XLVIII (January, 1950), 53-58.

Christmas Message, December 23, 1949. *Catholic Action,* XXXII (January, 1950), 3-5, 17.

"Social Function of Banking," Allocution to a Group of Directors and Employees of the Bank of Italy, April 25, 1950. *The Catholic Mind,* XLIX (May, 1951), 331-333.

"Vocation of Businessmen," Address to the Delegates of the World Congress of Chambers of Congress, April 27, 1950. *The Catholic Mind,* XLVIII (August, 1950), 510-511.

"Production for Human Needs," Address to Delegates to the Catholic International Congresses for Social Studies (Fribourg Union) and Social Action (Saint Gaul Union), June 3, 1950. *The Catholic Mind,* XLVIII (August, 1950), 507-510.

"Private Law and Its Co-ordination," Address to Two Hundred Jurists and University Professors at First International Private Law Congress, July 15, 1950. *The Catholic Mind,* XLVIII (December, 1950), 754-756.

Menti Nostrae, September 23, 1950. Washington: National Catholic Welfare Conference.

Christmas Eve Message, December 23, 1950. *The Catholic Mind,* XLIX (March, 1951), 201-208.

Address to Spanish Catholic Employers and Workers, March 11, 1951. *The Catholic Mind,* XLIX (October, 1951), 706-708.

Discourse to Delegates to the Fourth Congress of the World Movement for World Federal Government, April 6, 1951. *The Catholic Mind,* XLIX (June, 1951), 393-395.

Address to the First International Catholic Congress on Rural Problems, July 2, 1951. *The Catholic Messenger,* Davenport, Iowa, LXIX (July 19, 1951), 8.

Christmas Eve Address of 1951, December 24, 1951. *The Catholic Mind,* L (April, 1952), 248-256.

Address to Italian Catholic Association of Employers, January 31, 1952. *The Catholic Mind,* L (September, 1952), 569-572.

Letter to Charles Flory, President of Semaines Sociales de France, July 7, 1952. *The Tablet,* Brooklyn, New York, XLIV (August 9, 1952), 12.

Address to Members of the Austrian National Catholic Convention (Katholikentag), September 14, 1952. *The Catholic Messenger,* Davenport, Iowa, LXX (October 9, 1952), 14.

"The Moral Limits of Medical Research and Treatment," Address to the First International Congress on the Histopathology of the Nervous System, September 14, 1952. *The Catholic Messenger,* Davenport, Iowa, LXX (October 2, 1952), 3, 8.

Bibliography of the Industry Council Plan and Related Topics

Within each section, books and pamphlets—with titles capitalized—are given first; then, magazine articles with title or abbreviation of magazine capitalized.

An asterisk (*) indicates Catholic publication.

Some items could be classified under several headings but, in general, each item appears only once.

Abbreviations of Journals

ACSR	American Catholic Sociological Review	CER	Catholic Educational Review
AEcoR	American Economic Review	CM	Catholic Mind
		CSJ	Catholic School Journal
AER	American Ecclesiastical Review	COM	Commonweal
		HBR	Harvard Business Review
AJS	American Journal of Sociology	HPR	Homiletic and Pastoral Review
AM	Ave Maria		
AMER	America	ILR	International Labour Review
AM FED	American Federationist		
ANNALS	Annals of the American Academy of Political and Social Science	ILRR	International and Labor Relations Review
		IR	Interracial Review
ASR	American Sociological Review	IRQR	Industrial Relations Quarterly Review
CA	Catholic Action	L & N	Labor and Nation
CBER	Catholic Business Education Review	LIB	Labor and Industry in Britain

MLR	Monthly Labor Review	SF	Social Forces
MS	Modern Schoolman	SJR	Social Justice Review
RP	Review of Politics	SO	Social Order
RSE	Review of Social Economy	STU	Studies (Dublin)
		TS	Theological Studies
	YR	Yale Review	

CITED but not abbreviated: *C.I.O. News, Commentary, Fortune, Human Organization, Industrial Relations Research Assn. Proceedings, Journal of Electrical Workers and Operators, Measure, National Catholic Education Assn. Proceedings, New Republic, Plan Age, The Sign, Social Research, Survey, Thought, Today, World Today,* and *You and Industry.*

Section I—(1) *The Industry Council Plan*

* Arès, R. (T. P. Fay, trans.) WHAT IS CORPORATIVE ORGANIZATION? St. Louis: Central Bureau Press, 1939 (pam.).
* Azpiazu, J. THE CORPORATE STATE (W. Bresnahan, trans.). St. Louis: B. Herder Book Co., 1951.
* Bouvier, E. NEITHER RIGHT NOR LEFT IN LABOR RELATIONS. Montreal: University of Montreal, 1951.
* Bronson, R. A. THE ECONOMIC ORGANIZATION OF SOCIETY AND THE ENCYCLICALS. N.Y.: Paulist Press, 1937 (pam.).
  Bowen, Howard R. SOCIAL RESPONSIBILITIES OF BUSINESSMEN. (Chapter 12—ICP) N.Y.: National Council of Churches of Christ in the U.S.A., 1953.
* Bruehl, C. THE POPE'S PLAN FOR SOCIAL RECONSTRUCTION. N.Y.: Devin-Adair, 1939.
* Corrigan, J. M. LABOR'S RIGHT TO MANAGEMENT. Washington: Catholic University of America Press, 1948.
* Cronin, J. F. CATHOLIC SOCIAL PRINCIPLES. Milwaukee: Bruce Pub. Co., 1950.
* ———. CATHOLIC SOCIAL ACTION. Milwaukee: Bruce Pub. Co., 1948.
* Dempsey, B. W. CORPORATE DEMOCRACY. St. Louis: Central Bureau Press, 1941 (pam.).
* Donnelly, J. F. RECONSTRUCTING SOCIETY WITH CHRIST—Labor School Notes—Part Four (mimeographed). New Haven: Box 1224. 1950.
* Grenier, H. THOMISTIC PHILOSOPHY. Vol. III: Moral Philosophy, Chapter on "Professional Assns." Westminster, Md.: Newman Bookshop, 1950.
  Heron, A. R. BEYOND COLLECTIVE BARGAINING. Stanford: Stanford University Press, 1950.

* Higgins, T. J. MAN AS MAN. Appendix: "Occupational Groups." Milwaukee: Bruce Pub. Co., 1950.
* Husslein, J. C. DEMOCRATIC INDUSTRY. N.Y.: P. J. Kenedy & Sons, 1919.
* Industry Council Plan Committee of ACSS. PROS AND CONS OF PRICE AND OTHER CONTROLS UNDER THE ICP. (mimeographed). St. Louis: St. Louis University, 1950.
* ————. ANNUAL AND INTERIM REPORTS, 1947–53. St. Louis: St. Louis University.
* McGowan, R. A. NEW GUILDS: A CONVERSATION. N.Y.: Paulist Press (pam.).
* McLaughlin, T. HISTORY OF THE INDUSTRY COUNCIL PLAN COMMITTEE OF THE ACSS. Chicago: De Paul University, 1951. (unpublished M.B.A. thesis).
  Miller, W. A. CATHOLIC PLAN FOR A NEW SOCIAL ORDER. In Social Action 18: 3-43. Feb. 15, 1951. (Cong. Christian Churches & Evangel. & Reformed Church.)
* Muench, A. J. THE NEW SOCIAL ORDER. Fargo, N.D.: Bishop's House, 1941 (pam.).
* Munier, J. D. SOME AMERICAN APPROXIMATIONS TO PIUS XI's "INDUSTRIES AND PROFESSIONS." Washington: Catholic Univ. of America Press, 1943.
* National Catholic Welfare Conference. Labor Day Statements. Issued annually by the Social Action Dept. Washington: 1312 Massachusetts Ave., N.W.
* Nell-Breuning, O. v. REORGANIZATION OF SOCIAL ECONOMY (B. Dempsey, trans.). Milwaukee: Bruce Pub. Co., 1936.
* Raaijmakers, Muller, et al. THE GUILD SOCIAL ORDER. Oxford: Catholic Social Guild, 1936.
* Robert, Lambert. INDUSTRY COUNCILS: ANALYSIS OF THE MURRAY PLAN. St. Louis: St. Louis University, 1944. (unpublished Ph.D. dissertation.)
* Ryan, J. A. INDUSTRIAL DEMOCRACY FROM A CATHOLIC STANDPOINT. Washington: 1925.
* ————. A BETTER ECONOMIC ORDER. N.Y.: Harper, 1935.
* Serrarens, P. J. S. TOWARDS A SOCIAL ORDER. Washington: NCWC, 1952 (pam.).
* Trehey, H. F. FOUNDATIONS OF A MODERN GUILD SYSTEM. Washington: Catholic University of America Press, 1940.
* ————. WAR AND DEPRESSION. Our Remedy: Industrial Democracy. New Zealand, New Zealand Tablet, n.d.
* Walsh, J. P. BASIC PRINCIPLES OF THE INDUSTRY COUNCIL PLAN OF PIUS XI AND OF THE POLICY OF THE SHERMAN ACT. San Antonio: De Mazenod Scholasticate, 1951. Reprinted from RE-

vue de l'Université d'Ottawa, Jan.-Mar. & Apr.-June, 1951.
* ――――. The Industry Council Plan and the State. N.Y.: Industry Council Assn. Inc., 12 E. 41st St., 1951. (pam.)
* Ward, L. R. The American Apostolate—American Catholics in the Twentieth Century. (Chapter: Industrial Relations.) Westminster, Md.: Newman Press, 1952.
* Williams, L. The C.I.O. Industry Council Plan as an Approximation to Pius XI's Industries and Professions. Washington: Cath. Univ. of Amer. Press, 1951.

* Alter, Karl, Industry Councils. The Sign 29: 50-53, May 1950.
* Andrews, G. T. Order in Industrial Economy. MS 14: 56-58, March 1937.
* Annual Report of the Industry Council Plan Committee, ACSR 8: 285-89, Dec. 1947.
* Berna, J. B. Vocational Group Order. SO 1: 157-61, Nov.-Dec. 1947.
* Bruehl, C. Structure of the Vocational Group. HPR 38: 449-57, Feb. 1938.
* Catholic Universe Bulletin. 68: No. 26, Dec. 19, 1941.
* Cort, J. C. Plea for Economists. COM 47: 567-69, Mar. 19, 1948; Discussion, 48: 136, 141, May 21, 1948. See Cort's other columns in the Commonweal.
* ――――. Is a Christian Industrialism Possible? COM 49: 60, Oct. 29, 1948.
* Crane, P. Democratic Capitalism. STU (Dublin) 40: 33-46, Mar. 1951.
* Cronin, J. F. Some Approaches to an Industry Council Plan. CA 31: 6-7, Apr. 1949.
* ――――. Society and Freedom. CM 49: 686-93, Oct. 1951.
* Editorial: Capitalism Canonized? The Sign 29: Dec. 1950.
* Industrialism and Agrarianism—Official Statement of National Catholic Rural Life Conference. CM 47: 573-75, Sept. 1949.
* Industry Council Assn., Inc. The Sign 30: 6, Jan. 1951.
* Haas, F. J. Labor, Management, and Government. CM 47: 1-9, Jan. 1949.
* ――――. Three Economic Needs of the 1880's and the 1940's. AER 117: 401-25, Dec. 1947.
* ――――. Church Wants Planning on Basis of Mixed Economy. Journal of Electrical Workers and Operators. Pp. 128 ff., April, 1944.
* Higgins, G. G. American Contributions to the Implementation of the Industry Council Plan. ACSR 13: 10-24, Mar. 1952.
* ――――. Weekly syndicated column, "The Yardstick."

* Kelley, W. J. Industry Council Assn., Inc. ILRR 4: 627, July 1951.
* Land, P. S. & Klubertanz, G. P. Practical Reason, Social Fact, and the Vocational Order. MS 28: 239-66, May 1951.
* Marciniak, E. A. Debate on Christian Industrialism. TODAY, October 1949. Also, articles in WORK.
* McShane, J. Economic Democracy through V-Groups. SJR 36: 187-90, 231-33, 265-67, 304-66. Oct. Nov. Dec. 1943; Jan. 1944.
* Mueller, F. H. Genesis of the Vocational-Group Order. THE GUILDSMAN. Nov.-Dec. 1938; Jan.-Feb. 1939; Mar.-Apr. 1939; June-July 1949; Aug.-Sept. 1939; Oct.-Nov. 1939; Dec. 1939-Jan. 1940; Feb.-Mar. 1940; Apr.-May 1940; June-July 1940; Oct.-Nov. 1940.
* Nell-Breuning, O. v. The Social Structural order and European Economic Unity. RSE 10: 108-20, Sept. 1952.
* ———. Vocational Groups and Monopoly. RSE 9: 89-110, Sept. 1951.
* Parsons, W. What Are Vocational Groups? THOUGHT 17: 464-76, Sept. 1942.
* ———. Papal Plan for Social Reconstruction. CM 40: 1-9, Mar. 22, 1942.
* Schmiedeler, E. Pius XI's New Social Order and Agriculture. AER 103: 371-77, Oct. 1940.
* Schnepp, G. J. Survey of Opinions on the Industry Council Plan. ACSR 12: 75-83, June 1951.
* ———. A Catholic Industrial Program. CM 47: 489-99, Aug. 1949.
* ———. Let's Call It the Industry Council Plan. AMER 78:572-74, Feb. 21, 1948.
* Smith, W. J. The "Catholic" Viewpoint on Industry Councils. AER 122: 107-20, Feb. 1950.
Tead, O. Perspective on Democratic Industrial Government. ANNALS 224: 51, Nov. 1942.
* Tobin, T. J. Industry Councils. IR 22: 2, Jan. 1949.
* Weber, P. Economic Democracy. CM 40: 13-16, Aug. 22, 1942.

(2) *The Industry Council Plan—C.I.O.*

Congress of Industrial Organizations Pamphlets: (718 Jackson Place, N.W., Washington 6, D.C.)
No. 51: Philip Murray, THE CIO DEFENSE PLAN, 1941
No. 59: PLANNING FOR DEMOCRATIC DEFENSE, 1941
No. 64: Philip Murray, WE'LL WORK TO WIN, 1942
No. 67: WAR PRODUCTION, 1942

No. 83: Philip Murray, CHARTING THE VICTORY, 1943
No. 116: Philip Murray, CIO RE-EMPLOYMENT PLAN, 1944
Industry Council Plan Discussions, DAILY PROCEEDINGS of the
Tenth Constitutional Convention, C.I.O., Nov. 25, 1948, pp.
40-44. See other Convention Proceedings.

* Brophy, J. Industry Council Plan. COM 49: 110-12, Nov. 12, 1948.
Industrial Planning and Industry Councils. Social Action Notes,
March 1952.
Riordan, A. Murray First Advocated Industry Council Plan.
THE CIO NEWS 11: 6-7, Dec. 27, 1948.
Shelton, W. C. I. O.'s Own Revolution. NEW REPUBLIC 120:
7-8, Jan. 3, 1949.

SECTION II—(1) *The Church and Industry and Labor*

* Husslein, J. C. THE CHURCH AND INDUSTRIAL ASSOCIATIONS. St.
Louis: Central Bureau Press (pam.).
* Kenyon, R. THE CATHOLIC FAITH AND THE INDUSTRIAL ORDER.
London, P. Allan, 1931.
* Muench, A. J. THE CHURCH AND SOCIAL ORDER. Washington,
D.C.: NCWC, 1940 (pam.).
OUR CHURCHES AND LABOR-MANAGEMENT RELATIONS. New
Brunswick, N.J.: Institute of Management and Labor Relations,
Rutgers University, 1952.
* Welk, W. CURRENT PROGRAMS OF SOCIAL REFORM. St. Paul:
St. Thomas College Press (pam.).

Karson, M. The Catholic Church and the Political Development
of American Trade Unionism (1900-1918). ILRR 4: 527-42,
July 1951.
* Marciniak, E. The Church and Social Reform. TODAY, May 1951.
Mayer, M. P. The Catholic Church and the Union Movement.
L&N, Mar.-Apr. 1949.

(2) *Encyclicals and Commentaries*

* Brown, F. J. SOCIAL JUSTICE IN THE MODERN WORLD. Chicago:
Outline Press, Inc., 2308 W. Van Buren St., 1947 (pam.).
* Claudia, Sister Mary. GUIDE TO THE DOCUMENTS OF PIUS XII.
Westminster, Md.: Newman Bookshop, 1950.
* English, M., and Wade, W. L. REBUILDING THE SOCIAL ORDER.
Chicago: Loyola University Press, 1939.
* Hughes, P. THE POPE'S NEW ORDER. N.Y.: The Macmillan Co.,
1944.

* Husslein, J. C. SOCIAL WELLSPRINGS (2 vols.). Milwaukee: Bruce Pub. Co., 1940-2.
* ———. THE CHRISTIAN SOCIAL MANIFESTO. Milwaukee: Bruce Pub. Co., 1931.
* Keller, E. A. THE CHURCH AND OUR ECONOMIC SYSTEM. Notre Dame: University of Notre Dame, 1947 (pam.).
* McAulay, J. P. DIVINE PLAN FOR WORK AND WEALTH. Dublin: Clonmore & Reynolds, 1950.
* Michel, V. G. CHRISTIAN SOCIAL RECONSTRUCTION. Milwaukee: Bruce Pub. Co., 1937.
* Miller, R. J. FORTY YEARS AFTER. St. Paul: Radio Replies Press, 1947.
* Pope Leo XIII. ON THE CONDITION OF THE WORKINGMAN (RERUM NOVARUM), 1891.
* Pope Pius XI. ON THE RECONSTRUCTION OF THE SOCIAL ORDER (QUADRAGESIMO ANNO), 1931.
* ———. ATHEISTIC COMMUNISM (DIVINI REDEMPTORIS), 1937.
* Pope Pius XII. Labor's Dignity and Freedom. CM May 1949, 303-5.
* ———. Address to Catholic Employers. CM July 1949, 445-48.
* ———. Nobility of Work. CM Sept. 1949, 564-65.
* ———. Address of June 3, 1950. CM 48: 507-10, August 1950.
NOTE: See also Bibliography of Papal Documents, *supra*, pp. 197 to 202.
* Ryan, J. A. THE CONSTITUTION AND CATHOLIC INDUSTRIAL TEACHING. Washington: NCWC.
* Watt, L. A HANDBOOK OF RERUM NOVARUM. Oxford: Catholic Social Guild.
* ———. PIUS XI AND SOCIAL RECONSTRUCTION. Oxford: Catholic Social Guild.
* ———. NATIONALIZATION—WHAT THE POPE HAS SAID. Oxford: Catholic Social Guild.

* Abell, A. I. The Reception of Leo XIII's Labor Encyclical in America, 1891-1919. RP 7: 464-95, Oct. 1945.
* Baerwald, F. The Labor Encyclicals Today. THOUGHT 26: 165-79, Summer, 1951.
* CATHOLIC MIND 49, October 1951. Encyclical Anniversary Issue.
* Cronin, J. F. Economic Research and the Social Encyclicals: Progress and Poverty. RSE 10: 16-31, Mar. 1952.
* De Coursey, Sister M. E. Reconstruction of the Social Order. SJR 40: 149-53, Sept. 1947.
* Fenton, J. C. Religious Assent Due to the Teachings of Papal Encyclicals. AER 123: 59-67, July 1950. See also: AER 121: 136-50; 210-20; Aug.-Sept. 1949.

* Higgins, G. G. After Sixty Years. SO 1: 195-204, May 1951.
* Mueller, F. H. What the Encyclicals Do Not Teach. SJR 34: 43-45, May 1941.
* Mulcahy, R. E. Leading Industrialists Agree with the Encyclicals. AMER 61: 128-29, May 20, 1939.
* Schnepp, G. J. Social Progress, 1931-46—An Estimate of a Papal Document. ACSR 7: 3-14, Mar. 1946; CM 44: 661-70, Nov. 1946.

(3) *Catholic Hierarchy: Statements and Commentaries*

* Hierarchy of Canada. THE PROBLEM OF THE WORKER. Montreal: Palm Publishers, 470 St. Alexis St., 1950 (pam.).
* Hierarchy of the United States. THE CHURCH AND SOCIAL ORDER. N.Y.: Paulist Press, 1940 (pam.).
* Huber, R. M. (ed.). OUR BISHOPS SPEAK. Milwaukee: Bruce Pub. Co., 1952.
* NCWC Dept. of Social Action. THE INDUSTRIAL QUESTION AND THE BISHOP'S PASTORAL LETTER. Washington: NCWC, n.d. (pam.).

* Suhard, Emmanuel (Cardinal). PRIESTS AMONG MEN. N.Y.: Integrity Pub. Co., 243 E. 36th St. (pam.).
* Azpiazu, J. Social Attitudes of the Spanish Hierarchy. SO 1:75-79, Feb. 1951.
* Bishop Haas Offers Solution. AM 74: 548, Nov. 3, 1951.
* de Medeiros, R. S. Social attitudes of Brazilian Hierarchy. SO 1:23, Jan. 1951.
* Maher, F. Social Attitudes of the Australian Hierarchy. SO 1:115-22, Mar. 1951.
* Parsons, W. Social Thought of the American Hierarchy. SO 2: 259-78, June 1952.
* Villain, J. Social Attitudes of the French Hierarchy. SO 1: 257-68, June 1951.

SECTION III—*Principles*

* Ament, E. P. INDUSTRIAL RECOVERY LEGISLATION IN THE LIGHT OF CATHOLIC PRINCIPLES. Washington: Catholic University of America Press, 1936.
* Belloc, H. THE SERVILE STATE. London: T. N. Foulis, 1912.
  Chamberlain, N. LABOR'S RIGHT TO PARTICIPATE IN MANAGEMENT. New Haven: Yale University Press, 1948.
* Clump, C. C. THE ECONOMIC AND POLITICAL LIFE OF MAN. Oxford: Catholic Social Guild, 1947.
* Clure, G. CHRISTIAN SOCIAL REORGANIZATION. Dublin: Browne & Nolan Ltd., 1940.

* Commission on American Citizenship. BETTER MEN FOR BETTER TIMES. Washington: The Catholic University of America Press, 1943.

Commons, J. R. THE ECONOMICS OF COLLECTIVE ACTION (Parson, K. H., ed.). N.Y.: The Macmillan Co., 1950.

* Cronin, J. F. CATHOLIC SOCIAL PRINCIPLES. Milwaukee: Bruce Pub. Co., 1950.

Drucker, P. THE NEW SOCIETY. N.Y.: Harper and Bros., 1950.

———. THE FUTURE OF INDUSTRIAL MAN. N.Y.: John Day Co., 1942.

Ferre, N. F. S. CHRISTIANITY AND SOCIETY. N.Y.: Harper and Bros., 1950.

* Ferree, W. THE ACT OF SOCIAL JUSTICE. Dayton: Marianist Publications, 1951.

Girvetz, H. K. FROM WEALTH TO WELFARE. Stanford: Stanford Univ. Press, 1951.

Glueck, S. (ed.). THE WELFARE STATE AND THE NATIONAL WELFARE. Cambridge: Addison-Wesley Press, 1952.

* Gordon, A. SECURITY FREEDOM AND HAPPINESS. Oxford: Catholic Social Guild, 1944.

* Haas, F. J. MAN AND SOCIETY. N.Y.: Appleton-Century-Crofts, 1952.

* ———. RIGHTS AND WRONGS IN INDUSTRY. N.Y.: Paulist Press, 1933 (pam.).

Heermance, E. L. CAN BUSINESS GOVERN ITSELF? N.Y.: Harper and Bros., 1932.

* Hoffman, R. THE ORGANIC STATE. N.Y.: Sheed and Ward, 1939.

* International Union of Social Studies. A CODE OF INTERNATIONAL ETHICS. Oxford: Catholic Social Guild.

* ———. A CODE OF SOCIAL PRINCIPLES. Oxford: Catholic Social Guild.

* Jarrett, B. SOCIAL THEORIES OF THE MIDDLE AGES. Boston: Little, Brown, 1926.

* Land, P. S., Thomas, J. L., & Gavin, M. H. DEMOCRATIC LIVING. Chicago: Loyola University Press, 1952.

Lippincott, B. (ed.). GOVERNMENT CONTROL OF THE ECONOMIC ORDER. Minneapolis: University of Minnesota Press, 1935.

Lippmann, W. AN INQUIRY INTO THE PRINCIPLES OF THE GOOD SOCIETY. Boston: Little, Brown & Co., 1937.

* Manning, T. P. CONFLICT OR COOPERATION. N.Y.: Industry Council Assn., 1951 (pam.).

* Maritain, J. MAN AND THE STATE. Chicago: University of Chicago Press, 1951.

* Masse, B. L. ECONOMIC LIBERALISM AND FREE ENTERPRISE, N.Y.: America Press, 1944 (pam.).

* McGowan, R. A. TOWARD SOCIAL JUSTICE. N.Y.: The Paulist Press (pam.).

* McKevitt, P. THE PLAN OF SOCIETY. Dublin: Catholic Truth Society; N.Y.: Benziger Bros., 1944. (Contains summary of the Report of the Eire Commission.)

McLuhan, H. M. THE MECHANICAL BRIDE. N.Y.: Vanguard Press, 1951.

McMillon, H. THE MIDDLE WAY. N.Y.: The Macmillan Co., 1938.

* Messner, J. (J. J. Doherty, trans.) SOCIAL ETHICS. St. Louis: B. Herder, 1949.

* Mueller, F. H. HEINRICH PESCH AND HIS THEORY OF CHRISTIAN SOLIDARISM. St. Paul: College of St. Thomas, 1941 (pam.).

* Muench, A. J. ORGANIZED SOCIAL JUSTICE. N.Y.: The Paulist Press (pam.).

* Murray, R. W. SOCIOLOGY IN A DEMOCRATIC SOCIETY. N.Y.: Appleton-Century-Crofts, 1950.

* O'Brien, Mary Consilia. CHRISTIAN SOCIAL PRINCIPLES. N.Y.: P. J. Kenedy and Sons, 1941.

* Osgniach, A. MUST IT BE COMMUNISM? N.Y.: Joseph Wagner, Inc., 1950.

* Ostheimer, A., and Delaney, J. CHRISTIAN PRINCIPLES AND NATIONAL PROBLEMS. N.Y.: Sadlier, 1945.

Roepke, W. THE SOCIAL CRISIS OF OUR TIMES. Chicago: U. of Chicago Press, 1950.

————. CIVITAS HUMANA: A HUMANE ORDER OF SOCIETY. London: Hodge, 1948.

* Ryan, J. A. DISTRIBUTIVE JUSTICE. N.Y.: The Macmillan Co., 1942.

* ————. A BETTER ECONOMIC ORDER. N.Y.: Harper and Bros., 1935.

* Schwer, W. CATHOLIC SOCIAL THEORY. St. Louis: B. Herder, 1940.

* Somerville, H. WHY THE GUILDS DECAYED. N.Y.: The Paulist Press, 1938 (pam.).

* Thorning, J. F. A PRIMER OF SOCIAL JUSTICE. N.Y.: The Paulist Press, 1938 (pam.).

Tead, O. THE ART OF ADMINISTRATION. N.Y.: McGraw-Hill Book Co., 1951.

* WALSH, J. P. THE BASIC PRINCIPLES OF THE INDUSTRY COUNCIL PLAN OF PIUS XI AND OF THE POLICY OF THE SHERMAN ACT. San Antonio: De Mazenod Scholasticate, 1950.

* Clemens, A. H. Are Corporation Profits too High Judged by Christian Standards? SJR 43, Feb. 1950.

* Cronin, J. F. Pope Pius XII on Labor in Management. AMER 83: 461-63, Aug. 5, 1950.

Daugherty, C. R. Organized Labor and the Public Interest. YR, Spring 1950.

Dempsey, B. W. Roots of Responsibility. HBR 4: 393-402, July 1949.

* Diemer, A. Security Through Cooperation. SJR 38: 41-44, May, 1945.

* Dion, G. The Social Doctrine of the Church and the Economic Management of Enterprises. IRQR Sept. 1951.

Dubreuil, H. Industrial Organization on the Basis of Autonomous Groups. ILR 64: 285-302, Oct. 1951.

* Durbin, W. A. The Right Not to Join a Union. SO 2: 301-5, Sept. 1952.

Friedmann, G. Philosophy Underlying the Hawthorne Investigation. SF 28: 204-9, Dec. 1949.

* George, G. Priority of Means; Should Moral Reform Precede Social Reform? SO 1: 6-10, May 1947.

* Higgins, G. G. What Is Social Justice? CM 45: 561-62, Sept. 1947.

* Kelly, G. Notes on Moral Theology. Annual comment. TS, March issue.

* Kennedy, P. V. Civitas Humana (by W. Roepke). A review. SO 1: 224-26, May 1951.

* Land, P. S. Guides for social reform. SO 1: 100-6, Mar. 1951.

* McGowan, R. A. Social Justice and Sociology. ACSR 1: 68-73, June 1940.

* Messner, J. Freedom as a Principle of Social Order; an essay in the substance of subsidiary function. MS 28: 97-110, Jan. 1951.

* Mueller, F. H. Christian Solidarism and Labor. SJR 44: 3-6, April 1951.

* ———. What Is Solidarism? SJR 38: 298-301, Jan. 1946.

* Mulcahy, R. E. Social Justice: Responsibility of Management and Labor. CM 49: 500-3, August 1951.

* Ong, W. J. The Mechanical Bride (by H. M. McLuhan). A review. SO 2: 79-85, Feb. 1952.

* Parsons, W. Function of Government in Industry. MS 20: 63-71, Jan. 1943; CM 41: 7-15, Mar. 1943.

* Schuyler, J. Solidarism and Rural Life, SJR 37: May-June 1944.

* ———. Urban Society and Solidarism. SJR 44: 257-61, Dec. 1951.

* Smith, W. J. The Duty to Join a Union. SO 2: 387-391, Nov. 1952.

* Sturzo, L. The Philosophic Background of Christian Democracy, RP 9: 3-15, Jan. 1947.

* Thomas, J. L. Catholic Social Principles (by J. F. Cronin). A review. SO 1: 80-84, Feb. 1951.

* Timasheff, N. S. Nationalization in Europe and the Catholic Social Doctrine. ACSR 8: 111-30, June 1947.

SECTION IV—(1) *Labor-Management Co-operation*

Arnold, T. et al. THE FUTURE OF DEMOCRATIC CAPITALISM. Philadelphia: Univ. of Pennsylvania Press, 1950.

Atwater, F. S. et al. INDUSTRIAL ORGANIZATION AND MANAGEMENT. N.Y.: McGraw-Hill Book Co., 1945.

Bakke, E. W. BONDS OF ORGANIZATION. N.Y.: Harper and Bros., 1950.

———— and Kerr, C. UNIONS, MANAGEMENT AND THE PUBLIC. N.Y.: Harcourt, Brace and Co., 1948.

————. MUTUAL SURVIVAL. New Haven: Yale Univ. Press, 1946.

Barnard, C. I. ORGANIZATION AND MANAGEMENT. Cambridge: Harvard Univ. Press., 1948.

Bookbinder, H. H. & assoc. TO PROMOTE THE GENERAL WELFARE. N.Y.: Amalgamated Clothing Workers of America, 1950.

Bowen, H. R. TOWARD SOCIAL ECONOMY. N.Y.: Rinehart, 1950.

Braun, K. UNION-MANAGEMENT COOPERATION. Washington: Brookings Institute, 1947.

Briefs, G. THE PROLETARIAT. N.Y.: McGraw-Hill Book Co., 1937.

CAUSES OF INDUSTRIAL PEACE. 15 case studies. Washington: National Planning Assn., 800 21st St. N.W. (6).

Chamberlain, N. W. UNION CHALLENGE TO MANAGEMENT CONTROL. N.Y.: Harper, 1948.

Chase, S. et al. SOCIAL RESPONSIBILITY OF MANAGEMENT. N.Y.: New York University, 1951.

Clegg, H. A. LABOR RELATIONS IN LONDON TRANSPORT. N.Y.: Aug. M. Kelley, 1950.

CODE OF ETHICS AND PROCEDURAL STANDARDS FOR LABOR-MANAGEMENT ARBITRATION. N.Y.: American Arbitration Assn., 9 Rockefeller Plaza (20).

Cooke, M. L. and Murray, P. ORGANIZED LABOR AND PRODUCTION. N.Y.: Harper, 1940.

COOPERATION BETWEEN PUBLIC AUTHORITIES AND EMPLOYERS' AND WORKERS' ORGANIZATIONS. Washington: International Labor Office, 1825 Jefferson Pl., N.W., 1951.

COOPERATION IN INDUSTRY. Washington, Intl. Labor Office, 1952.

* Corrigan, J. L. MANAGEMENT AND MANAGEMENT'S RIGHTS TO MANAGE IN INDUSTRIAL RELATIONS. Washington: Catholic Univ. of America Press, 1950.

Dubin, R. HUMAN RELATIONS IN ADMINISTRATION. N.Y.: Prentice-Hall, 1951.

Gardner, B. B. HUMAN RELATIONS IN INDUSTRY. N.Y.: R. D. Irwin Co., 1946.

Golden, C. S. and Ruttenberg, H. J. THE DYNAMICS OF INDUSTRIAL DEMOCRACY. N.Y.: Harper and Bros., 1942.

GREATER PRODUCTIVITY THROUGH LABOR-MANAGEMENT COOPERATION. N.Y.: American Management Assn., 1950.

Harbison, F. H. and Dubin, R. PATTERNS OF UNION-MANAGEMENT RELATIONS. Chicago: Science Research Associates, 1947.

Heron, A. TOWARD UNDERSTANDING IN INDUSTRY (3 vols.). Stanford: Stanford University Press, 1947-48.

* Hogan, W. T. PRODUCTIVITY IN THE BLAST-FURNACE AND OPEN-HEARTH SEGMENTS OF THE STEEL INDUSTRY: 1920-1946. N.Y.: Fordham Univ. Press, 1950.

HUMAN RELATIONS IN MODERN BUSINESS. N.Y.: Prentice-Hall, 1949 (pam.).

International Labour Office. LABOR-MANAGEMENT COOPERATION IN U.S. WAR PRODUCTION. Montreal: ILO, 1948.

Johnson, R. W. PEOPLE MUST LIVE AND WORK TOGETHER, OR FORFEIT FREEDOM. N.Y.: Doubleday and Co., 1947.

* Kenkel, J. B. SHARING THE PROFITS WITH EMPLOYEES. Washington: NCWC (pam.).

* Kerwin, J. G. MAKING DEMOCRACY WORK. N.Y.: Paulist Press, 1939.

Kuzer, D. M. & assoc. MAKING CAPITALISM WORK. N.Y.: McGraw-Hill Book Co., 1950.

Lester, R. E. & Shister, J. INSIGHTS INTO LABOR ISSUES. N.Y.: Macmillan, 1948.

Lever, E. J. LABOR MANAGEMENT COOPERATION. N.Y.: Harper and Bros., 1948.

Lewison, S. A. HUMAN LEADERSHIP IN INDUSTRY. N.Y.: Harper and Bros., 1945.

Luckman, C. WHERE FREEDOM BEGINS. Cambridge: Lever Bros. Co., 1952.

McCabe, D. A. LABOR AND SOCIAL ORGANIZATION. Boston: Little, Brown & Co., 1938.

* McGinley, J. J. LABOR RELATIONS IN THE NEW YORK RAPID TRANSIT SYSTEM. N.Y.: Columbia Univ. Press, 1949.

Merrett, H. F. (ed.) RESPONSIBILITY OF BUSINESS LEADERSHIP. Cambridge: Harvard Univ. Press, 1948.

Miller, G. W. AMERICAN LABOR AND THE GOVERNMENT. N.Y.: Prentice-Hall, 1948.

Monsees, C. H. INDUSTRY-GOVERNMENT COOPERATION. N.Y.: Public Affairs Press.

Nichols, O. PARTNERS IN PRODUCTION: A BASIS FOR LABOR-MANAGEMENT UNDERSTANDING. N.Y.: Twentieth Century Fund, 1949.

* O'Shaughnessy, M. ECONOMIC DEMOCRACY AND PRIVATE ENTERPRISE. N.Y.: Harper, 1945.

PATTERN FOR ECONOMIC JUSTICE. Catholic, Protestant, & Jewish Declaration. Washington: NCWC.

Peters, R. W. COMMUNICATION WITHIN INDUSTRY: PRINCIPLES AND METHODS OF MANAGEMENT-EMPLOYEE INTERCHANGE. N.Y.: Harper and Bros., 1950.

Richberg, D. GOVERNMENT AND BUSINESS TOMORROW. N.Y.: Harper and Bros., 1943.

Roethlisberger, F. J. MANAGEMENT AND MORALE. Cambridge: Harvard U. Press, 1941.

——— and Dickson, W. J. MANAGEMENT AND THE WORKER. Cambridge: Harvard Univ. Press, 1939.

* Schuyler, J. CHRISTIAN SOLIDARISM AND LABOR MANAGEMENT COMMITTEES OF WORLD WAR II. St. Louis: St. Louis University, 1945 (unpublished M.A. thesis).

Selekman, M. LABOR RELATIONS AND HUMAN RELATIONS. N.Y.: McGraw-Hill Book Co., 1947.

Seward, W. TEAMWORK IN INDUSTRY. N.Y.: Funk and Wagnalls, 1950.

Slichter, S. H. THE CHALLENGE OF INDUSTRIAL RELATIONS. Ithaca: Cornell Univ. Press, 1947.

———. UNION POLICIES AND INDUSTRIAL MANAGEMENT. Washington: Brookings Institution, 1941.

Stern, F. M. CAPITALISM IN AMERICA. N.Y.: Rinehart and Co., 1951.

Stewart, M. S. THE AMERICAN WAY—BUSINESS FREEDOM OR GOVERNMENT CONTROL? Washington: Public Affairs Press, 1947 (pam.).

Strong, J. V. EMPLOYEE BENEFIT PLANS IN OPERATION. Washington: Bureau of National Affairs, Inc., 1951.

Tannenbaum, F. A PHILOSOPHY OF LABOR. N.Y.: Alfred A. Knopf, 1951.

* Toner, J. L. THE CLOSED SHOP IN THE AMERICAN LABOR MOVEMENT. Washington: Catholic Univ. of America Press, 1941.

Wilcox, W. CAN INDUSTRY GOVERN ITSELF? N.Y.: Norton, 1931.

Whyte, W. F. PATTERN FOR INDUSTRIAL PEACE. N.Y.: Harper and Bros., 1951.

* Ahner, A. A. Human Labor Relations. SO 1: 107-10, March 1951.
* Brown, L. J. Profit Sharing Pays. SO 1: 65-74, Feb. 1951.

Davenport, R. Enterprise for Everyman. FORTUNE 41: 55-59, Jan. 1950.

Dixon, R. G. Tripartism in the National War Labor Board. ILRR 2:372-90, April 1949.

Dubin, R. Union-Management Cooperation and Productivity. ILRR 2: 195-209, Jan. 1949.

Duddy, E. A. Authority and Responsibility of Business. MEASURE (H. Regnery Co., 20 West Jackson Blvd., Chicago 4, Ill.).

Efficiency in Privately-Owned Industry. LIB 5: 83 ff., April 1947.

* Frommelt, H. A. Christianizing Industrial Management. SIGN 19:40-42, Aug. 1939.

Goldberg, A. J. Civil Rights in Labor-Management Relations: A labor viewpoint. ANNALS: 275: 148-54, May 1951.

* Higgins, G. G. Labor-Management Committees. CM 43: 96-97, Feb. 1945.

Joint Production Committees. LIB 5: Nos. 7, 8, 9 (1947).

Labor in the American Economy. ANNALS 274, Issue of March 1951.

Labour-management Cooperation in the Undertaking (France, England, U.S. and Canada). ILR 59: 192-205, Feb. 1949.

* Labor Monopoly. I.S.O. Forum. SO 1:73-82, June 1947.

* Masse, B. L. Labor and Management. AMER 85:32 April 14, 1951.

* ———. Labor-management Relations. VITAL SPEECHES 14: 498-99, June 1, 1948.

* McShane, J. L. Labor-management Cooperation. SO 1: 129-32, Sept.-Oct. 1947.

National Association of Manufacturers. Employer-Employee Cooperation. YOU AND INDUSTRY, No. 11, 1943.

November, H. Industry Committees under the Fair Labor Standards Act. AM FED 47: 271-80, Mar. 1940.

Roethlisberger, F. J. Human Relations: Rare, Medium, or Well-done? HBR 26: 89-107, Jan. 1948.

Schuyler, J. Story of the L-M C's. SIGN 24: 406-7, Mar. 1945.

Tead, O. Advancing the Public Interest in Labor Relations. ILRR 2: 391-402, April 1949.

Wickenden, E. The People's Unfinished Business. SURVEY 88: 7-11, Jan. 1952.

* Wilken, R. Labor Unions Today. SJR 39: 189-94, Oct. 1946.

Willauer, P. B. Civil Rights in Labor-Management Relations: A Management Viewpoint. ANNALS 275: 140-47, May 1951.

(2) *Collective Bargaining*

Carpenter, J. T. EMPLOYERS' ASSOCIATIONS AND COLLECTIVE BARGAINING IN NEW YORK CITY. Ithaca: Cornell Univ. Press, 1952.

Chamberlain, N. W. COLLECTIVE BARGAINING. N.Y.: McGraw-Hill Book Co., 1951.

Cheyfitz, E. T. CONSTRUCTIVE COLLECTIVE BARGAINING. N.Y.: McGraw-Hill Book Co., 1947.

Davey, H. W. CONTEMPORARY COLLECTIVE BARGAINING. N.Y.: Prentice-Hall, 1951.

Dickinson, Z. C. COLLECTIVE WAGE DETERMINATION. N.Y.: Ronald Press, 1941.

Harbison, F. H., and Coleman, J. R. GOALS AND STRATEGY IN COLLECTIVE BARGAINING. N.Y.: Harper and Bros., 1951.

Lazarus, H., and Goldberg, J. COLLECTIVE BARGAINING. Washington: Public Affairs Institute, 1949. Report No. 3.

Peck, G. (ed.). FACTORS IN SUCCESSFUL COLLECTIVE BARGAINING. Washington: Government Printing Office, 1951.

Pollack, O. SOCIAL IMPLICATIONS OF INDUSTRY WIDE BARGAINING. Philadelphia: Univ. of Pennsylvania Press, 1948.

Randle, C. W. COLLECTIVE BARGAINING. Boston: Houghton Mifflin Co., 1951.

Twentieth Century Fund. MODERN TRENDS IN COLLECTIVE BARGAINING. N.Y.: Twentieth Century Fund, 1947.

Witney, F. (ed. by J. Shister.) GOVERNMENT AND COLLECTIVE BARGAINING. Philadelphia: J. B. Lippincott, 1951.

Peterson, F. Management Efficiency and Collective Bargaining. ILRR 1: 29-49, Oct. 1947.

Selekman, B. M. Living with Collective Bargaining. HBR 20: 21-33, Autumn 1941.

(3) *Planning*

MacKenzie, F. (ed.) PLANNED SOCIETY, YESTERDAY, TODAY, AND TOMORROW. N.Y.: Prentice-Hall, 1937.

Mannheim, K. FREEDOM, POWER, AND DEMOCRATIC PLANNING. N.Y.: Oxford University Press, 1950.

Wooton, Barbara. FREEDOM UNDER PLANNING. Chapel Hill: Univ. of North Carolina Press, 1945.

Can Capitalism Plan? ANNALS 162, July 1932.

Lederer, E. National Economic Planning. ENCYCLOPEDIA OF THE SOCIAL SCIENCES.

Cole, G. D. H. PRINCIPLES OF ECONOMIC PLANNING. N.Y.: Macmillan Co., 1935.

Galloway, G. B. PLANNING FOR AMERICA. N.Y.: Holt, 1941.

———. INDUSTRIAL PLANNING AND THE CODES. N.Y.: Harper, 1935.

SECTION V—*Legislation*

Bailey, S. K. CONGRESS MAKES A LAW (Full Employment Act of 1946). N.Y.: Columbia Univ. Press, 1950.

Bouvier, E. A DISCUSSION ON PENSION PLANS. Montreal: University of Montreal, 1951 (pam.).

————. UNEMPLOYMENT INSURANCE IN CANADA, 1940-1950. Montreal: University of Montreal, 1951 (pam.).

Gregory, C. O. LABOR AND THE LAW. N.Y.: Macmillan, 1946.

* Higgins, G. G. Union Attitudes Towards Economic and Social Roles of the Modern State. Reprinted from INTERPRETING THE LABOR MOVEMENT. Champaign: Industrial Relations Research Assn., 1952. Pp. 149–70.

Taylor, G. W. GOVERNMENT REGULATION OF INDUSTRIAL RELATIONS. N.Y.: Prentice-Hall, 1948.

SECTION VI—*Sociological Aspects*

Jaques, E. THE CHANGING CULTURE OF A FACTORY. N.Y.: Dryden Press, 1952.

* Lerhinan, J. P. A SOCIOLOGICAL COMMENTARY ON "DIVINI REDEMPTORIS." Washington: Catholic Univ. of America Press, 1946.

Mayo, E. THE SOCIAL PROBLEMS OF AN INDUSTRIAL CIVILIZATION. Cambridge: Harvard Univ. Press, 1945.

Meadows, P. THE CULTURE OF INDUSTRIAL MAN. Lincoln: Univ. of Nebraska, 1950.

Miller, D. C., and Form, W. H. INDUSTRIAL SOCIOLOGY. N.Y.: Harper & Bros., 1951.

Moore, W. E. INDUSTRIAL RELATIONS AND THE SOCIAL ORDER. N.Y.: Macmillan Co., 1951.

Rose, A. M. UNION SOLIDARITY. Minneapolis: Univ. of Minnesota Press, 1952.

Walker, C. R., and Guest, R. H. THE MAN ON THE ASSEMBLY LINE. Cambridge: Harvard Univ. Press, 1952.

Warner, W. L., and Low, J. O. THE SOCIAL SYSTEM OF THE MODERN FACTORY. THE STRIKE: A SOCIAL ANALYSIS. Yankee City Series, Vol. IV. New Haven: Yale Univ. Press, 1947.

Weber, M. THE THEORY OF SOCIAL AND ECONOMIC ORGANIZATION. N.Y.: Oxford Univ. Press, 1947.

Whyte, W. F. INDUSTRY AND SOCIETY. N.Y.: McGraw-Hill, 1946.

Babchuk, N., and Goode, W. J. Work Incentive in a Self-determined Group. ASR 16: 679-87, Oct. 1951.

Bendix, R. Bureaucracy: The Problem and Its Setting. ASR 12: 493-507, Oct. 1947.

Blumer, H. Sociological Theory in Industrial Relations. ASR 12: 271-78, June 1947.

Dunlop, J. T., and Whyte, W. F. Framework for the Analysis of Industrial Relations. ILRR 3: 383-412, April 1950.

* Fitzpatrick, J. P. Catholic Responsibilities in Sociology. THOUGHT 26: 384-96, Autumn 1951.

* ———. Industrial Sociology: Contributions and Confusions. ACSR 12: 138-47, October 1951.
* ———. The White Collar Worker and Wall Street. ACSR 9: 98-107, June 1948.

Homann, G. C. Strategy of Industrial Sociology. AJS 54: 330-37, Jan. 1949.

* Kerins, J. L. The Catholic Sociologist and the Sociology of Industry. ACSR 8: 12-23, March 1947.

Kleeck, M. v. Towards an Industrial Sociology. ASR 11: 501-5, Oct. 1946.

Mayo, E. Psychiatry and Sociology in Relation to Social Disorganization. AJS 42: 825-31, May 1937.

Mills, C. W. The Contributions of Sociology to the Study of Industrial Relations. PROCEEDINGS, INDUSTRIAL RELATIONS RESEARCH ASSN., Champaign: 1949.

Moore, W. E. Industrial Sociology: Status and Prospects. ASR 13: 382-400, August 1948.

* Mueller, F. H. The Social Question of the Shop. ACSR 9: 84-97, June 1948.

Schneider, E. V. Limitation on Observation in Industrial Sociology. SF 28: 279-84, March 1950.

Sheppard, H. L. Treatment of Unionism in "Managerial Sociology." ASR 14: 310-13, April 1949.

The Sociology of Work. Issue of AJS, March 1952.

Stead, W. H. Democracy and Social Controls in Industry. ASR 7: 177-84, 1942.

* Wilken, R. Foremen Unions and the Labor Movement. SJR 37: 39-42, May 1944.

Worthy, J. C. Organization Structure and Employee Morale. ASR 15: 169-79, April 1950.

Whyte, W. F. Patterns of Interaction in Union-management Relations. HUMAN ORGANIZATION 8: 13-19, Fall 1949.

SECTION VII—*Economic Aspects*

Allen, G. H. INDIVIDUAL INITIATIVE IN BUSINESS. Cambridge: Harvard Univ. Press, 1950.

* Baerwald, F. FUNDAMENTALS OF LABOR ECONOMICS. N.Y.: Declan X. McMullen, 1947.

* Bardes, G. F. DISTRIBUTION OF PROFITS IN THE MODERN CORPORATION. Washington: Catholic Univ. of America Press, 1951.

Bloom, G. F., and Northrup, H. R. ECONOMICS OF LABOR AND INDUSTRIAL RELATIONS. Philadelphia: Blakiston Co., 1950.

Boulding, K. A RECONSTRUCTION OF ECONOMICS. N.Y.: Wiley & Sons, 1950.

Council of Economic Advisers. Annual Reports. Washington: U.S. Government Printing Office.

* Cronin, J. F. ECONOMIC ANALYSIS AND PROBLEMS. N.Y.: American Book Co., 1945.

Economic Reconstruction. N.Y.: Columbia Univ. Press, 1934.

* Flubacher, J. F. THE CONCEPT OF ETHICS IN THE HISTORY OF ECONOMICS. N.Y.: The Vantage Press, 1950.

* Land, P. S. PROLEGOMENA TO ECONOMIC COMMUNITIES. St. Louis: St. Louis University, 1950 (unpublished Ph.D. dissertation).

* Mulcahy, R. THE ECONOMICS OF HEINRICH PESCH. N.Y.: Henry Holt & Co., 1952.

Nourse, E. G. THE 1950's COME FIRST. N.Y.: Henry Holt & Co., 1951.

Orton, W. A. THE ECONOMIC ROLE OF THE STATE. Chicago: Univ. of Chicago, 1950.

Schumpeter, J. THEORY OF ECONOMIC DEVELOPMENT. Cambridge: Harvard Univ., 1936.

Shister, J. (ed.). READINGS IN LABOR ECONOMICS AND INDUSTRIAL RELATIONS. Philadelphia: J. P. Lippincott Co., 1951.

Stein, E. (ed.). LABOR IN A MOBILIZATION ECONOMY. Proceedings of N.Y.U. Fourth Annual Conference on Labor. Albany: Matthew Bender Co., 1951.

Wright, D. M. CAPITALISM. N.Y.: McGraw-Hill Book Co., 1951.

Yoder, D. LABOR ECONOMICS AND LABOR PROBLEMS. N.Y.: McGraw-Hill Book Co., 1939.

* The Enterprise. SO Issue of May 1952.

* Gundlach, G. Solidarist Economics. SO 1: 181-85, April 1951.

* Keller, E. A. The Church and Our Economic System. AM 65: 263-66, 303-8, 338-41. March 1, 8, and 15, 1947.

Kreps, T. A National Economic Council for the U.S. PLAN AGE 2, Dec. 1936.

* Land, P. S. Capitalism: Toward a Humane Economic Order. SO 1: 412-21, Nov. 1951. Comment by Wright, rejoinder by Land: SO 2: 141-43, March 1952.

Lederer, E. National Economic Councils. ENCYCLOPEDIA OF THE SOCIAL SCIENCES.

* Masse, B. L. Pope Pius XII Demands Economic Reforms. AMER 84:378-80, Dec. 30, 1950.

* Mueller, F. H. Rejecting Right and Left; Heinrich Pesch and Solidarism. THOUGHT 26: 485-500, December 1951.

* Mulcahy, R. E. Economic Freedom in Pesch. SO 1: 161-68, April 1951.

* Nell-Breuning, O. v. The Peschian Interest Theory. SO 1: 177-80, April 1951.

Sawyer, J. E. Social Structure and Economic Progress. AEcoR 41: 321-9, May 1951.

* Solterer, J. Quadragesimo Anno: Schumpeter's Alternative to the Omnipotent State. RSE 9: 12-23, March 1951.
* Yenni, J. Pesch's Goal of the Economy. SO 1: 169-76, April 1951.

SECTION VIII—(1) *Countries Other Than the U.S.*

Bowen, R. H. GERMAN THEORIES OF THE CORPORATIVE STATE WITH SPECIAL REFERENCE TO THE PERIOD 1870-1919. N.Y.: McGraw-Hill Book Co., 1947.

Derrick, M. THE PORTUGAL OF SALAZAR. London: Sands, 1938.

EIRE REPORT. Commission on Vocational Organization. Dublin: The Stationery Office, 1943.

* Gouin, L. M. INTRODUCTION TO THE STUDY OF THE NEW GUILD SYSTEM. Social Bulletin No. 2. Montreal: L'Ecole Sociale Populaire, 1940 (pam.).

* Clarke, W. N. Industrial Democracy in Belgium. SO 2: 48-68, Feb. 1949; and ACSR 10: 229-57, Dec. 1949.
* de Bruin, P. Toward Economic Order (Netherlands). SO 1: 54-64, Feb. 1951.
* Einaudi, M. Christian Democracy in Italy. RP 9: 16-33, Jan. 1947.
* European Industrial Councils. SO 1: 229-31, Jan.-Feb. 1948.
* Jarlot, G. The Beginnings of Neo-Corporatism in France. MS 16: 12-15, Nov. 1936.

Joint Committees in Belgium; Legal Recognition. ILR 53: 81-82, Jan. 1946.

* Portugal's Corporative System. SJR 44: 126-27, July 1951.
* Schroeder, E. F. Toward Industrial Democracy in Holland. AMER 79: 328-29, July 10, 1948.
* Solzbacher, W. Plant Councils in Belgium. AMER 83: 418-20, July 22, 1950.

(2) *Codetermination, Cogestion, Etc.*

* Atar, A. P. German Labor Leads the Way. SIGN: July 1951.
* Brown, L. C. Labor-management Cooperation. SO 1: 211-23, May 1951.

Codetermination. NEWSWEEK 40: 45-46, Oct. 13, 1952.

* Co-Management in Germany. CM 49: 13-16, Jan. 1951.
* Cronin, J. F. Social Exchange Today. SO 1: 435-39, Dec. 1951.
* Desautels, A. R. and Fallon, J. M. Social Achievements in Belgian Industry, SO 1: 361-66, Oct. 1951.
* Economic Joint-management. AMER 83: 459, Aug. 5, 1950. Discussion: 83: 568, Sept. 2, 1950; 83:660, Sept. 23, 1950.

Fisher, P. Labor Codetermination in Germany. SOCIAL RESEARCH 18: 449-85, December 1951.

Herschel, W. Employee Representation in the Federal Republic of Germany. ILR 64: 207-15, August 15, 1951.

* Kellermann, A. F. Labor's Demand for Codetermination in German Economy. St. Louis U., MA, 1952.

* Lauer, Q. Co-Management in Germany. SO 1: 11-22, Jan. 1951.

Managerial Revolution in Western Germany. WORLD TODAY 7: 249-62, June 1951.

* Masse, B. L. Labor's Right in Management. AMER 83, July 15, 1950.

McPherson, W. H. Codetermination. ILRR 5: 20-32, October 1951.

Mitbestimmungsrecht. TIME 60: 27, August 4, 1952.

Mitbestimmungsrecht. FORTUNE 43: 54, April 1951.

* Nell-Breuning, O. v. Comment on Lauer's article in Jan. 1951 issue of SOCIAL ORDER. SO 1: 287-88, June 1951.

* Solzbacher, W. Codetermination Problem in Germany. AMER 83: 463-66, Aug. 5, 1950.

* Thomas, J. L. Codetermination and the European worker. ACSR 13: 146-58, Oct. 1952.

Weigert, O. Codetermination in Western Germany. MLR 73: 649-56, Dec. 1951.

SECTION IX—*Teaching*

* Bedier, Sr. M. Juliana. NEIGHBORS IN ONE WORLD (8th grade text). N.Y.: W. H. Sadlier, Inc., 1952.

* Jude Aloysius, Bro. CHRIST CENTERED HIGH SCHOOL SOCIOLOGY. SOME TEACHER AIDS. Winona, Wis.: Cotter High School, 1950.

* LABOR IS A PARTNER. St. Paul: Catechetical Guild, 1949.

* Sloyan, G. S. CHRISTIAN CONCEPTS IN SOCIAL STUDIES IN CATHOLIC EDUCATION. Washington: Catholic Univ. of America Press, 1951.

Ware, C. F. LABOR EDUCATION IN UNIVERSITIES. N.Y.: American Labor Education Service, 1776 Broadway, 1946.

* CBER, Issue of Nov. 1950, 2: No. 1. J. F. Noll, Need for social order; Bro. Justin, Economic liberalism; J. F. Cronin, Economics and the moral law; C. B. Aziere, Christian concept of property; W. J. Hart, Problems of labor; J. W. Leslie, Problems of management; E. J. Lodge, Savings and profit-sharing pension fund.

* CBER, Issue of Feb. 1951, 2, No. 2. W. J. Smith, Labor unions; J. Q. Adams, Employers associations; W. E. Brown, Problems of management; W. C. Speers, Labor-management relations; G. J. Schnepp, Industry Council Plan; J. P. Walsh, Industry Council

Plan and the State; E. A. Marciniak, Approaches to the Industry Council Plan; W. C. Downing, Integrating socio-economic principles in the teaching of history; R. J. Miller, Integration of Catholic social principles.

* Celine, Sr. Mary. Teaching the Labor Encyclicals in the Primary Grades. CSJ 52: 227-28, Sept. 1952.
* Donnelly, J. F. Social Teaching in the Schools. CM 49: 420-22, July 1951.
* Downing, W. Q. A. in the Classroom. AMER 81: 604-5, Sept. 10, 1949.
* Feeney, W. H. Social Teaching in Jamaica. SO 2: 110-14, March 1952.

Herberg, W. When Social Scientists View Labor. COMMENTARY Dec. 1951 (available from American Jewish Committee, 34 E. 33rd St. N.Y. 1, N.Y.).

* Higgins, G. G. Catholic Social Principles in the Modern World. CBER 3: 23-32, April 1952.
* Justin, Bro. Study of Industrial and Labor Relations in Catholic Colleges. CM 48: 719-24, Dec. 1950.
———. Story of Industrial and Labor Relations in Catholic Colleges. ILRR 3: Oct. 1949.

Kerrison, I. L. H. WORKERS' EDUCATION AT THE UNIVERSITY LEVEL. New Brunswick: Rutgers University Press, 1951.

Liveright, A. A. UNION LEADERSHIP TRAINING. N.Y.: Harper and Bros., 1951.

* McGowan, R. A. Social Encyclicals in the Schools. CA 22: 15, Oct. 1940.
* Miriam Therese, Sr. Presenting Basic Christian Principles in High School Sociology. ACSR 12: 84-93, June 1951.
* ———. Integrating the Papal Encyclicals in Shorthand and Transcription Classes. CBER 3: 33-37, April 1952.
* Ryan, L. V. Youth and the Social Encyclicals. CER 22: 306-8, Feb. 1952.
* Teaching Christian Social Living in the Elementary School and in the Upper Grades. NCEA PROCEEDINGS (1950) 47: 419-36, 1950.
* Twomey, L. J. Papal Social Teaching in Business Education. CM 48: 669-72, Nov. 1950. Also in: CBER 3: 51-57, April 1952.
* ———. Social Challenge to Education. SO 1: 105-7, Sept.-Oct. 1947.
* Vincent Ferrer, Sr. Mary. Principal Points a Teacher Should Stress in the Labor Encyclicals. NCEA PROCEEDINGS (1947) 44: 404-10, 1947.

SECTION X—*Miscellaneous*

Beard, C. A., and Smith, G. H. E. THE FUTURE COMES. A Study of the New Deal. N.Y.: The Macmillan Co., 1933.

Clark, J. M. ALTERNATIVE TO SERFDOM. N.Y.: Alfred A. Knopf, 1948.

Harris, S. (ed.) SCHUMPETER, SOCIAL SCIENTIST. Cambridge: Harvard Univ., 1951.

* Smith, W. J. SPOTLIGHT ON LABOR UNIONS. N.Y.: Duell Pub. Co., 1946.

* ———. WHAT IS THE CATHOLIC ATTITUDE? N.Y.: America Press, 1945 (pam.).

* ———. GOD, THE WORLD AND THE CATHOLIC WORKINGMAN. Huntington, Ind.: Our Sunday Visitor Press, 1940.

Whyte, W. H. IS ANYBODY LISTENING? N.Y.: Simon and Schuster, 1952.

* Briefs, G. Pesch and his contemporaries. SO 1: 153-60, April 1951.

Catholic Labor Priests. FORTUNE, Jan. 1949.

* Engelen, W. Henry Pesch, S.J. SJR 19 (1926).

* SOCIAL ORDER. Issue of April 1951, 1: No. 4. Heinrich Pesch.

SECTION XI—*Bibliographies*

Bibliographies will be found in many of the works listed in this bibliography. Here we merely call attention to a few of them, and to several not prevously listed.

* Arès, R. (T. P. Fay, trans.) WHAT IS CORPORATIVE ORGANIZATION? St. Louis: Central Bureau Press, 1939 (pam.).

* Cronin, J. P. CATHOLIC SOCIAL PRINCIPLES. Milwaukee: Bruce Pub. Co., 1950.

INDUSTRIAL RELATIONS ABSTRACTS AND ANNOTATIONS. Published monthly by the New York State School of Industrial and Labor Relations, Cornell University, Ithaca, N. Y.

* Institut Sociale Populaire. BIBLIOGRAPHIE CORPORATIVE. Montreal: 25 Jarry St. West.

LABOR'S LIBRARY (annotated bibliography). N.Y.: Workers Education Bureau, American Federation of Labor, 1440 Broadway (18).

Moore, W. E. INDUSTRIAL RELATIONS AND THE SOCIAL ORDER. N.Y.: Macmillan, 1951.

* Mulcahy, R. E. BIBLIOGRAPHY of the works of Heinrich Pesch. SO 1: 186-92, April 1951.

* SOCIAL ORDER. Annual bibliography of the Industry Council Plan, beginning with April 1953 issue.

* Messner, J. SOCIAL ETHICS. St. Louis: B. Herder Book Co., 1949.
* Walsh, J. P. BASIC PRINCIPLES OF THE INDUSTRY COUNCIL PLAN OF PIUS XI AND OF THE POLICY OF THE SHERMAN ACT. San Antonio: De Mazenod Scholasticate, 1951.

SECTION XII—*Publications* not elsewhere listed which periodically carry articles pertinent to the Industry Council Plan

* AD USUM SACERDOTUM. Laval University, Quebec, Can.
  AMERICAN FEDERATIONIST. (A F of L). Washington, D.C.
* BULLETIN. Hartford Diocesan Labor Institute, Box 1224, New Haven, Conn.
* THE COOPERATOR. Industry Council Assn., Inc., 12 East 41st St., New York, N.Y.
* CROWN HEIGHTS COMMENT. 1150 Carroll St., Brooklyn 25, N.Y.
  ECONOMIC OUTLOOK (CIO). 718 Jackson Place NW, Washington 6, D.C.
* THE GUIDEPOST. Boston College Business School, Chestnut Hill 67, Mass.
* Hayes, J. EVERYBODY'S BUSINESS. Weekly column in ALAMO REGISTER, San Antonio, Tex.
* INDUSTRIAL RELATIONS. Laval University, Quebec, Can.
* INSIGHT. St. Joseph's College, 18th & Thompson Sts., Philadelphia 21, Pa.
  LABOR LAW JOURNAL, 214 N. Michigan Ave., Chicago 1, Ill.
* THE LABOR LEADER (ACTU), 327 Lafayette St., New York 12, N.Y.
* LABOR MANAGEMENT PANEL. University of San Francisco, San Francisco 17, Cal.
* THE MEDIATOR. Catholic Labor Institute, 970 Third Ave., Los Angeles 6, Cal.
  NOTES. National Council of Churches, 297 Fourth Ave., New York 10, N. Y.
* SOCIAL ACTION BULLETIN. Saint Louis Archdiocesan Labor Institute, 5239 West Florissant Ave., Saint Louis 15, Mo.
* SOCIAL ACTION NOTES FOR PRIESTS. Social Action Dept., NCWC, 1312 Massachusetts Ave. NW, Washington 5, D.C.
* WAGE EARNER (ACTU), 58 West Adams, Detroit, Mich.
* WORK. Catholic Labor Alliance, 21 W. Superior, Chicago 10, Ill.

SECTION XIII—*Organizations* which study and promote ideas directly or indirectly related to the Industry Council Plan. It is to be noted that many colleges are omitted here.

* L'Action Corporative, 25 Jarry St. West, Montreal 14, Can.

American Management Assn., 50 Memorial Drive, Cambridge 39, Mass.

* Assn. of Cath. Trade Unionists, 327 Lafayette, N.Y.; 58 W. Adams, Detroit, Mich.

* Cath. Business & Professional Men's Club, 329 W. Main St., Louisville, Ky.

* Catholic Labor Alliance, 21 W. Superior, Chicago 10, Ill.

* Catholic Labor Institute, 970 Third Ave., Los Angeles 6, Calif.

* Clergy-Industry Discussion Group, 3055 Colerain Ave., Cincinnati 25, O.

Committee for Economic Development, 444 Madison Ave., New York 22, N.Y.

* Catholic Business Education Assn., % St. Benedict's College, Atchison, Kan.

* Catholic Economic Assn., % Marquette University, Milwaukee, Wis.

* Council of Cath. Orgs. for Social Order, Manhattan College, N.Y.

Council of Profit-Sharing Industries, First National Tower, Akron 8, O.

* Diocesan Labor Institute (Hartford Dioc.), Box 1224, New Haven 5, Conn.

Industrial Relations Center, Univ. of Wisconsin, Madison, Wis.

Industrial Relations Research Assn., 704 S. Sixth St., Champaign, Ill.

* Industrial Research Center, 25 Jarry St. West, Montreal 14, Can.

* Industry Council Assn. Inc., 12 East 41st St., New York, N.Y.

* Industry Council Plan Committee, Amer. Cath. Sociological Soc., Saint Louis University, 221 N. Grand, St. Louis 3, Mo.

* Institute of Ind. Relations, College of the Holy Cross, Worcester 10, Mass.

* Institute of Ind. Relations, % St. Ann's Parish, Manchester, N.H.

Institute of Management and Labor Relations, Rutgers Univ., New Brunswick, N.J.

* Inst. of Social and Ind. Relations, Loyola Univ., 820 N. Michigan, Chicago 11, Ill.

* Institute of Social Education, St. John College, Cleveland, O.

* Institute of Social Order, Rockhurst College, Kansas City, Mo.

* Institute of Social Order, 221 N. Grand Blvd., St. Louis 3, Mo.

* Institut Sociale Populaire, 25 Jarry St. West, Montreal 14, Can.

International Labor Office, Montreal, Can.

* Labor Management School, Univ. of San Francisco, San Francisco 17, Cal.

* Catholic auspices.

* LeMoyne College School of Industrial Relations, Rochester, N.Y.
* National Council of Catholic Men, 1312 Massachusetts Ave., N.W., Washington 5, D.C.
* National Council of Catholic Women, 1312 Massachusetts Ave. NW, Washington, D.C.
* National Federation of Catholic College Students.
  National Planning Assn., 800 21st St. N.W., Washington 6, D.C.
* Newman Clubs.
* St. Peter's College Institute of Industrial Relations, Jersey City, N.J.
* St. Vincent College Sociology Department, Latrobe, Pa.
* Social Action Dept., NCWC, 1312 Massachusetts Ave. N.W., Washington 5, D.C.
* Social Order Forum, 980 Park Ave., New York, N.Y.

Index

Documents are indexed under the key words assigned to each. For complete identification of the document, see Key to Documents Cited, pp. 192 ff., and Bibliography, pp. 197 ff.

This book may be kept

FOURTEEN DAYS

A fine will be charged for each day the book is kept overtime.

GAYLORD 142			PRINTED IN U.S.A.